National and International	*Region...*
May:	
Germans announce death of Hitler. Unconditional surrender of all German forces. VE Day in Britain. Channel Islands liberated. UK coalition government resigns and Churchill forms "caretaker" administration. Rangoon recaptured. Dutch royal family returns home. Norwegian government returns to Oslo.	Towns and villages celebrate V.E. End of black-out. First USAAF groups leave for home. German E-boats sail to Felixstowe to to surrender. 50-year "Plan for Norwich" published. USAAF subscribe £20,000 for American library at Norwich. Essex battalion aids relief operation in Netherlands.
June:	
Charter of United Nations signed at San Francisco. Simla conference to consider constitutional changes in India. Organised Japanese resistance on Okinawa ceases. King and Queen visit Channel Islands.	Evacuated school-children return to to London. First boats decommissioned by Navy resume fishing from East Coast ports. Scandinavian timber ships return. General Election campaign.
July:	
Attlee, after general election victory, forms Labour government in UK. Potsdam conference of Allied leaders. Philippines liberated. US warships bombard Japan. Allied Control Commission takes over government of Berlin.	Sweeping Labour gains throughout the region. Royal Navy closes its base at Great Yarmouth. Heavy landings of trawl fish at East Coast ports.
August:	
Atomic bombs dropped on Hiroshima and Nagasaki. Russia declares war on Japan. Japan surrenders unconditionally. VJ Day in Britain. British Parliament approves United Nations Charter. Russo-Polish frontier treaty announced. British naval force occupies Hong Kong.	VJ celebrations everywhere. First news of East Anglians liberated from Japanese prison camps. Cambridge confers Freedom on 300,000 USAAF men. GI Brides Club formed in Norwich. Most US bomb groups leave—bases opened to public. League football resumed—8,186 at first Norwich City match.
September:	
US Lend-Lease terminated. MacArthur's forces enter Tokyo. Mountbatten receives Japanese surrender in SE Asia at Singapore. New plan for India announced. Japanese surrender Hong Kong. Dockers strike in UK.	Harvest gathered and Italian POW's begin to leave farms. German POW's deployed on farms and building sites. Liberation of POW camps in Far East; East Anglian survivors assembled for return to UK.

EAST ANGLIA 1945

Overleaf: Hale Street Victory Party, Cambridge. *Cambridgeshire Collection*

EAST ANGLIA 1945

by

R. DOUGLAS BROWN

TERENCE DALTON LIMITED
LAVENHAM   .   SUFFOLK
1994

Published by
TERENCE DALTON LIMITED

ISBN 086138 102 5

Text photoset in 10.5/12pt Times

Printed in Great Britain at
The Lavenham Press Limited, Lavenham, Suffolk

Contents

Publishers' Note

The publishers regret that the reproduction of certain illustrations is below the quality that they would normally demand. The *East Anglian Daily Times* and the *Eastern Daily Press*, who kindly permitted us the use of their files, were unfortunately unable to provide original photographs and, consequently, the pictures shown are reproductions from the printed newspapers. The same applies to those photographs from the *Cambridge Evening News* that were so kindly provided by the Cambridge Collection of the Cambridgeshire Libraries. Where applicable, it was considered preferable to show illustrations, even if below our usual standard, rather than no pictures at all.

To David
who arrived in 1945

Index of Illustrations

Introduction and Acknowledgements

THIS VOLUME – the seventh in a series – completes the story of the experience of the people of East Anglia during the period 1939 to 1945, the years of the Second World War. I have aimed throughout at an objective and comprehensive account of events, using only contemporary source material and avoiding long-term reminiscences—which are often selective and embroidered. Many other accounts of the war have made it entirely a saga of thrills and excitement. The people of East Anglia certainly experienced that aspect of war, particularly when under threat of invasion and during the Battle of Britain in 1940. But they also learned that war can be dull and dispiriting, a time of boredom and frustration, of loneliness and privation. I have sought to describe the whole of life as it was, day by day, the hardship and unhappiness as well as the melodrama.

In East Anglia a few thousand people were killed. It is estimated that in the warring nations as a whole, more than thirty million people died—no one will ever be able to arrive at a reliable figure. Never before in history had so many people been taken from their homes and set to tasks of destruction; never before had so much destruction been carried out; and never before had the social fabric and the economic structure of so many nations been permanently undermined. An American airman who flew from an East Anglian base afterwards wrote of "the impersonal fury of destruction" and "the incredible brutality and inhumanity" in which he had been involved"[1].

The best that can be said is that men of goodwill felt forced into the hostilities by circumstances over which they had lost control. The Prussian general Karl von Clausewitz argued that war is the continuation of diplomacy by other means and so it has been. Put another way, it is the last resort of statesmen who have failed in their primary responsibility to settle conflict and dispute by negotiation. The irony is that the statesmen rarely pay a price for their failures, which are camouflaged by loading all blame on the other party and then insisting upon "national unity". In the words of the American airman already quoted, the faces of statesmen on a winning side then "hang alongside the portraits of saints and [are] only a little less honoured."

In this final volume East Anglia is observed during the transition from war to peace. The people, faced with the task of building a new post-war society, showed as clear a sense of purpose and as great a determination to succeed as they had done during the war years—but in 1945, uniquely, they themselves set the agenda. Again they faced a long and painful struggle.

The present generation of East Anglians confronts a new challenge. The Europe from which once came the threat of armed invasion is now the Europe where opportunity lies for Great Britain as a partner in a twenty-first century

Renaissance. Success in this enterprise will be the surest safeguard that the experiences of the Second World War will never be repeated.

The daily life of the people of the eastern counties during 1945 was faithfully recorded in the regional newspapers, and I have drawn freely on their news reports, feature articles, photographs and advertisements. I wish to thank the Eastern Counties Newspapers Group Ltd, Cambridge Newspapers Ltd and the editors of the various newspapers for permission to make use of this material.

A more intimate insight into the circumstances of the time is offered by the documents held in the Mass Observation archive at Sussex University, personal diaries and replies to questionnaires sent out by the MO organization. I thank the custodians of the archive for permission to quote from these documents, and Ms Dorothy Sheridan, BA, the archivist, and her assistants for their guidance.

I am indebted to the publishers of the official histories of the three East Anglian regiments for permission to quote extensively from their accounts of engagements in which the regiments took part. I have consulted a number of other military histories, and these are acknowledged in the text.

For a picture of life on the American air bases in East Anglia I am grateful in particular to the Reverend James Good Brown, whose wonderfully detailed narrative in *The Mighty Men of the 381st: Heroes All* has the rare virtue of having been compiled day by day, as events unfolded. I have a special debt of gratitude to Mr Ian Hawkins, Mr Dave Osborne and Mr Jock Whitehouse, who supplied many photographs of RAF and USAAF activities.

I wish to express appreciation of the co-operation of staff at the Department of Photographs at the Imperial War Museum, the Public Record Office at Kew, the Local Studies Department of the Norfolk County Library at Norwich, the Suffolk Record Office at Bury St Edmunds and Ipswich, and the Cambridgeshire Local History Collection at Cambridge Central Library.

The various volumes of the official war history published by Her Majesty's Stationery Office have provided the broader background of the war, and they have been supplemented by Sir Winston Churchill's personal account, *The Second World War*, and by the volumes based on the Churchill papers produced by Mr Martin Gilbert: *Second World War* and *Road to Victory—Winston Churchill 1941–1945*.

Detailed acknowledgements will be found in the notes on sources at the end of the book.

Stoke-by-Clare, Suffolk.
April 1992.   R. DOUGLAS BROWN

ISSUED BY THE MINISTRY OF FUEL AND POWER

GAS and ELECTRICITY

WARNING

Ice-bound coal trains and road transport, an unprecedented strain on gas works and power stations — those were the consequences of the recent abnormal weather. It will take time for coal stocks to recover from the effects of these conditions.

All consumers must make a special effort to cut down their consumption of gas and electricity at home and in the works, in offices, in shops, restaurants and hotels. This must be done not only in the interests of economy but in order to enable stocks to be built up again as rapidly as possible.

From industry an all-round cut of 10% has been asked. Maximum economies must be made in domestic consumption. The increase in domestic demand has been marked even in areas which have suffered little or no bomb damage.

ONLY THE MOST DRASTIC ECONOMY WILL ENABLE WAR PRODUCTION TO BE CARRIED ON AT FULL PRESSURE.

CHAPTER ONE

The Road out of Darkness

A WIND whetted like a scythe and louring clouds laden with Arctic snow stormed in from the North Sea and enveloped the coastal areas of East Anglia. A foot of snow fell overnight in the seaside resort of Cromer. All traffic came to a standstill. On the farms it took strong men all their time and energy to struggle to the livestock with feed. They could do little else; sugar beet and potatoes were frozen into the ground and there was no possibility of drilling winter wheat. The military were called in to help to get things moving again, and by the end of January the worst blizzard for thirty years had blown itself out.

During this bitter weather there was a serious shortage of fuel. People anxiously switched on their radio sets each morning to hear whether the 7 am BBC news bulletin included a warning of electricity cuts. If overload of the grid was threatened listeners were urged to switch off as many appliances as possible. Even so, the eastern counties had no supply for fifteen minutes at breakfast-time on 24th January and for an hour three days later. No one escaped these cuts, not even hospitals or factories.

Most homes depended upon coal for heating, and the shortage was acute. Many had had none delivered since October—with Norwich and King's Lynn among the worst affected. Troops and army vehicles handled coal supplies in London. Even after the weather improved and the worst of the difficulties were overcome, the ban on heating shops, offices, blocks of flats and places of entertainments remained in force until 31st October. In most respects, however, the situation was transformed within three months. The eastern counties enjoyed a memorable spring-time, the most beautiful anyone could remember. On one particularly balmy March day the temperature in Norwich reached 65.7 degrees. Flowers blossomed in cottage gardens, and on the farms spring seeding was completed early and harvest prospects were excellent.

There was a consonance between the contrasting seasons and the fluctuating moods of leaders and people during these opening months of 1945. This was to be a year of despair as well as a year of hope. It became a year of horror as continents were ravaged, but also a year of joy as fighting ended. The American president,

The Ministry of Fuel's "Gas and Electricity Warning" was part of the ceaseless drive for economy.
Cambridge Daily News

Roosevelt, greeted it optimistically: "This new year can be the greatest year of achievement in human history . . . 1945 can and must see the substantial beginning of the organisation of World Peace." A few weeks later Prime Minister Winston Churchill remarked to his daughter Sarah: "I do not suppose that at any moment in history has the agony of the World be so great or widespread. Tonight the sun goes down on more suffering than ever before."[1]

The *Eastern Daily Press* was right to assert in a leading article published on New Year's Day that the people of East Anglia might be confident that the long and bloody war would soon be over, but that that was not going to end their problems. "More and more clearly the war emerges as an incident in a great upheaval of which nobody can foresee the end", the newspaper declared. Though the region was on the periphery of the most convulsive events that lay ahead, it would find itself inextricably linked to them in countless ways.

The January weather had far-reaching consequences. The same bitter temperatures that stopped the factories in Ipswich and Peterborough threatened frostbite for the men of several East Anglian regiments posed for an advance across the German frontier. It stopped most of the bombers taking off from East Anglian bases to continue the relentless assault of the German heartland. It added to the anxieties of those responsible for convoying supplies at great risk from the United States, for any short-fall of crops produced on the farms of Norfolk, Suffolk and Essex would have to be made up from that quarter. Those supplies were in doubt in any case; the *Eastern Daily Press* published what it termed "disquieting" reports that shipments of meat from the United States were to be cut for three months during the spring to only one-eighth of the current supply.

Much of the talk of housewives as they queued in the food shops was of how best to stretch the meagre rations. Churchill told the Commons on 21st March that the total food stocks of the United Kingdom were six million tons, but by the end of June they would be down to 4,750,000 tons — "no more than is necessary to maintain a regular flow of distribution under present conditions".

"Existing conditions" were not good, as William Stock, a hospital worker lodging in Chelmsford, noted in his diary:

> My landlady finds the food problem more difficult now than at any previous period of the war. Meat has been in short supply this week. She said this morning: "If I can't get any fish, I don't know what I shall give you to eat tonight." However, she got some fish. There is a scarcity of rice, potatoes and meat. I think most people accept the fact that the people of Europe are much worse off than we are and need food more than we do. At the same time, everybody thinks we have had more than enough of rationing.[2]

A few days later he was cock-a-hoop because his landlady had given him grapefruit for breakfast – the first he had had during the war. It called for front-page headlines in the local newspaper when there were:

LEMONS FOR COLCHESTER AREA

From time to time there were minor adjustments of the rations, as when in April the weekly milk allowance for adults was increased from 2½ to three pints a week—for a period of twelve weeks only. Soon after that, however, the Minister of Food announced ration cuts, which he attributed to world shortages. The weekly bacon ration was reduced from four to three ounces, cooking fats were reduced from two to one ounce, shredded suet was brought into rationing, and soap supplies (except for babies) were cut by one-eighth. Butchers were required to take one-seventh of their supplies in canned corned beef. Even with these reductions Britain began to draw heavily on stocks.

Clothing as well as food was still strictly rationed. At the beginning of the year the Board of Trade issued twenty-four clothing coupons to each adult, but the minister, Mr Hugh Dalton, was unable to tell the Commons the period they would have to cover. He hoped there would be more coupons for use from 1st August, but it would depend upon "the heavy and increasing demands" made by the services on labour and materials, including their need to have clothing ready for those who were demobilized.

With rationing so tight, ration books acquired great value and attracted the attention of criminals. The Food Office at Newmarket was burgled and seventeen

Cambridge's only woman bus driver, working for Eastern Counties. *Robin Goodfellow* the CDN columist, wrote: "All will agree that this driver is to be congratulated on her pluck in tackling the traffic of Cambridge".
Cambridge Daily News

thousand clothing coupons were stolen, while at Colchester three men diverted fifteen thousand clothing coupons into illicit channels.

The general run of crime was not a major problem at this time. The Chief Constable of Cambridgeshire, Mr W. H. Edwards, reported indictable offences down in a year from 571 to 460. Misdemeanours in Norwich had increased only slightly—by about eight per cent—and drunkenness was at its lowest level since 1919. The Chief Constable of East Suffolk was less happy, however, reporting that the 1,988 indictable offences known to the police was the highest total ever recorded—but they included many cases of theft of bicycles, a common wartime offence everywhere.

One feature of all the chief constables' reports was concern about juvenile delinquency. In Cambridge, it was stated, some mothers were neglecting their children; and a great deal of juvenile delinquency was due to unhappy homes from which the fathers were absent. "These children will certainly suffer in the years to come", the Cambridge police chief declared. An increase in juvenile delinquency in Norwich was also attributed to lack of parental control. One hundred and five children and young persons had been before the courts there during the year, thirty more than during the previous year.

The Cambridge Borough Chief Constable, Mr B. N. Bebbington, told the Cambridge Women Citizens' Association in January that his officers had "a great deal of trouble" with married women who had lost the idea of remaining true to their husbands. During the war many single girls made loving relationships with visiting servicemen, which often led to happy marriages; but there was also a great deal of promiscuity which ended in unhappiness.

The Bishop of Norwich, Dr P. M. Herbert, quoted in his *Diocesan Gazette* letters he had received from two army officers serving overseas, asserting that an increasing number of homes were being broken up owing to the infidelity of wives.

A colonel in the Norfolk Regiment serving in the Far East wrote that he had just had reported to him two more cases of wives having illegitimate children, and he enquired whether anything was being done "to impose a restraining influence on the men who are seducing the wives of soldiers serving away from home". The second letter came from a chaplain serving with the Mediterranean forces:

> Cases of unfaithful wives are very widespread and in some units may be calculated as being as high as one in ten. These cases largely concern women who have been married, and happily married, for a number of years ... it is impossible to describe the mental and moral devastation caused to a husband when he hears of his wife's infidelity. It cuts the ground completely from under him.

The chairman of the North East Suffolk branch of the St Edmundsbury and Ipswich Diocesan Moral Welfare Association, the Reverend Howard Dobson, declared that "the moral slump does not appear at all to have abated" and its organizing secretary, Miss Ashby, foresaw serious post-war problems. Some promiscuity was blatant. A Bury St Edmunds lady noted in her diary early in 1945:

> A man near us in Guildhall Street had an American visitor recently at midnight, who . . .
> wanted a room for the night. He was drunk and carried a bottle half-full of whisky. Being
> refused the bed, he said he wanted a woman and would pay five pounds for one. Wasn't this
> the bad part of the town? The householder pretended a police sergeant lived there and called
> upstairs to him, and the American then made off . . .[3]

There were many more brothels in East Anglia than ever before, and they were not only in the larger towns. There were regular prosecutions for prostitution, particularly in Cambridge, a favourite leave town. In a typical case in January a mother was sent to prison and her two daughters were fined for keeping a brothel regularly visited by black American servicemen. Later in the year a Thetford hotel-keeper was fined one hundred pounds for permitting his premises to be used as a brothel.

During the summer girls camped out in a hut across the road from an American camp in Milton Road, Cambridge. A sentry at the camp shot through the heart and killed a thirty-seven-year-old woman who failed to stop when challenged as she was leaving during the early hours. Two teenage girls who spent three weeks in the hut were brought to court accused of stealing US army blankets.

Cases of women accused of performing abortions came before the courts regularly. Occasionally the pregnant woman had died; in one such case a Cambridge woman was imprisoned for two years and her accomplice bound over. Many thousands of illegitimate children were born in the region during the war years*.

During the early months of 1945 East Anglia still faced danger from enemy action. V1 "buzz-bomb" rockets had been exploding across the region since the previous June, and those who lived near the coast had grown accustomed to the pounding of anti-aircraft guns aiming to bring them down before they reached populated areas. The gunners were achieving remarkable successes by the turn of the year—they shot down sixty or seventy off Harwich and Felixstowe during the last twelve days of December. Many still got through. One exploded on the Brightlingsea marshes early in January, shattering scores of windows and causing other minor damage.

The V1 "buzz-bomb" was an unpleasant weapon. One could watch its relentless advance towards an unknown and indiscriminate target. It was very noisy and it trailed a tail of flame. An American observer recorded this impression of one:

> It was not very high up and was travelling very fast. It made a terrific roar . . . . When it
> crossed directly over me it was "spitting". All of a sudden, the engine went "bl-l-l-l-up, bl-l-l-

---

*See *East Anglia 1943*, page 136 for statistics. By the time the war ended three hundred thousand illegitimate children had been born in Great Britain since the outbreak – three times the pre-war rate – and of these about seventy thousand had been fathered by GIs. East Anglia had its full share.

Telephone : KENSINGTON 9066 (Four Lines)   Telegrams : "LANSETTLER, SOUTHKENS, LONDON."

THE LAND SETTLEMENT ASSOCIATION LTD.

Registered under the Industrial and Provident Societies Acts, 1893-1928

Chairman :
THE EARL OF ELGIN and KINCARDINE, K.T., C.M.G. LL.D., T.D.   The Hyde,
Vice-Chairmen : A. C. Richmond   W F Stiff   Great Yeldham,
Hon. Treasurer : F. E. Dodson   Essex.

Executive Committee
The Chairman   The Lord Phillimore M C
The Vice-Chairmen   Professor R. Rae, B Agr
The Hon. Treasurer   John H. Robinson,
Sir Percy Alden, M.A.   Sir John Russell, O.B.E., D.Sc., F.R.S.   (Close to South Kensington Station).
Colonel G. R. Crosfield, C.B.E.   Miss D. S. Tomkinson
Mrs. Walter Elliot,   D.S.O., T.D.   I Wilkie, M.A   In your reply please quote reference :—

Controller : A. C. Richmond   CB/AB/YEL.16A.

{ Asst. Controllers : G. E. Owen (Secretary).
  Dr. C. Burgess, Ph.D (Production and Marketing)   23rd. February 1945.

                    The Chief Engineer,
                    U.S.A.A.F.,
                    Ridgewell,
                    Essex.

        Dear Sir,
                      I shall be obliged if you can arrange for
        the part of a plane to be removed from No. 52, Tilbury Road, Great.
        Yeldham, Essex. The plane crashed on 21st. January 1945, and a
        large part of it fell quite close to the dwelling house of one of
        my employees', almost blocking the entrance to the house.

                    Yours Faithfully,

                        C. Baker.
                     (C.Baker)
                      ESTATE MANAGER.

There were many plane crashes in East Anglia. This letter from an Estate Manager dated 23rd February requests the removal of wreckage from private property.

Dave Osborne

lop, bl-l-l-umph." The engine shut off entirely. The plane went into a straight nose-dive . . . When it hit, there was a huge column of smoke. The sky overhead was filled with black, ugly smoke. I rode as fast as I could to the village of Clare, a short distance away. The plane had crashed just outside the center of the community. I hurried to the vicar's house. The Rev Mr Swithinbank was at the door to greet me. With a calm smile on his face, he said "That was just one of those buzz bombs—quite a nuisance they are."[4]

For a few months the V1s were launched from German bombers which carried them piggy-back over the North Sea. This method was abandoned in mid-January, and a few weeks later the Germans launched a new version of the "buzz-bomb" from ramps in Holland. Relief came after 29th March, a day on which four exploded in the region—at Datchworth in Hertfordshire, and at Great Holland, Great Wigborough and Little Oakley in Essex. The one at Little Oakley damaged the church, two farms and thirty-one houses. The last sight of a V1 in East Anglia was at Orfordness, when one was shot down into the sea by AA guns at 12.43 pm.[5]

Beside the V1s there were V2 rockets, twenty-three of which landed in the region during January. These did even more damage—one which fell at Halstead on 13th January damaged 280 houses—and they introduced an entirely new experience. Because they travelled faster than the speed of sound there was no warning of their approach; the sound of their passage through the air was heard *after* the explosion. One at Clacton on 22nd January caused twenty-seven casualties and damaged 207 houses; another at Chelmsford the following day killed one person, injured sixteen and damaged 227 houses. Another landed on the seafront at Clacton and badly damaged a number of hotels, including the Grand

and the Towers, and many shops. Searchlights were used in the rescue operations and a number of people were taken to hospital. The last V2 landed on 27th March.

Reports in the press of all these incidents placed them in "Southern England"; it was judged that any more definite location would have helped the German crews who were despatching them across the North Sea.

Luftwaffe bombers reappeared over East Anglia in March, the first time for almost a year. On 4th March high explosives fell on Seymour Road, Ipswich, killing nine people and demolishing half a dozen houses. Other HE bombs fell at Botesdale, Colchester, Docking, East Rudham, Fulmodestone, Great Bromley, Little Cressingham, Rendlesham and Rickinghall and in the countryside around Swaffham. The following night Beccles was bombed and the Germans shot down an RAF Mosquito over Potter Heigham in Norfolk. The raiders swooped low and strafed random targets with machine-gun fire, including Everards Hotel and the Playhouse in Bury St Edmunds, and villages over a wide area.

The Luftwaffe attacks were now usually concentrated on airfields. Sixty bombers arrived on 3rd March, seeking concealment in a stream of returning Allied bombers, and for nearly five hours they roamed widely and attacked thirty RAF and USAAF bases in Norfolk and Suffolk. Six of the raiders were destroyed. During another night the airfields at Coltishall, Swanton Morely, Swannington and Metfield were targeted, one bomb exploding on the main runway at Metfield. A particularly daring German pilot flew his Junkers plane under a USAAF Liberator when it was on its final approach to Metfield. He miscalculated, tried to extricate himself in a tight turn, brushed a wing-tip along the ground, and crashed. Surrounding areas were often machine-gunned in the course of these raids, as at Swaffham, Wickham Market and Dereham.

The last night activity over East Anglia was during the evening of 20th March, when single planes cruised over the whole region, again devoting their attention to airfields, and the last German bomb on Norfolk hit Swanton Morely airfield at 9.30 pm that day.

Besides the V1s, V2s and Luftwaffe bombers there was another hazard. The skies were so full of British and American planes that inevitably there were accidents. Examples during the early weeks of the year were at Norwich when two children were killed and another injured when a low-flying US Liberator touched the gable end of a house in Spynke Road and crashed in the garden where they were playing; and near Ely when two planes collided in mid-air. Two more children were killed when one crashed at Prickwillow.

The end of the German air assault coincided with a magnificent spring. The severe wintry spell gave way to warm and sunny days when the temperature exceeded any known in England at this time of year for fifty years. A newly arrived American noted "weather that seemed too good to be true—day after day the sun shone bright and clear, a warm wind blew"[6].

The sun was shining, too, on the western front. An officer with the East Anglian battalions there noted in the midst of battle "new buds on the fruit-trees in gardens where snowdrops grew" and, as they moved to cross the Rhine, "a fine warm day like early summer . . . the sky was blue, turning gold . . .".

Hope was in the air, and in the eastern counties some of the tensions of life were eased. On 4th April a Chelmsford diarist noted: "There have been no rockets or flying bombs over Easter and people who have been sleeping downstairs are speaking of going upstairs again . . ."[7].

The arriving American GI already quoted seemed enchanted by his life in the region:

> One of the most pleasant places in Bury was the Forces' Study Centre . . . in a pleasant house of rambling passages and old oak beams, operated by the British Army Educational Corps . . . There was at least one good concert a week, attended by both the troops and the townspeople; there were classes in German and in French, in carpentry and wood-working and toy-making, in sketching and painting; a play-reading group met once a week to read Shakespeare, Sheridan, Wilde, and Shaw; there were discussion groups and listening groups; and on Saturday afternoons and Sundays there were excursions to points of interest in the neighbourhood . . . There was an activity of interest every night of the week.[8]

In Cambridge a pre-war custom was resumed at St John's College when its choir sang from the chapel tower on Ascension Day. There was no shortage of leisure and pleasure activity in Cambridge at this time, and all tastes were catered for. There was a four-week season of Christmas pantomime at the Arts Theatre. Kathleen Ferrier gave a song recital to the Cambridge Music Society. The Royal

The Suffolk Agricultural Association Spring Stallion Show at Ipswich in March.

East Anglian Daily Times

The Cambridge firm of Joshua Taylor offered a reclamation service for tennis balls.

Cambridge Daily News

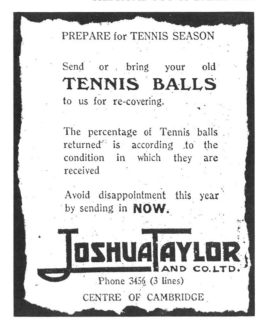

Canadian Air Force Headquarters Band gave a concert at the Guildhall. Most week nights there were dances at the Dorothy Cafe and at the Rex Ballroom; on one occasion the BBC Television Dancers visited the Guildhall to demonstrate the latest ballroom dances, including "The Jive". The Cambridge Film Society presented such classics as Flaherty's *Man of Aran*.

The cinema was the most popular diversion, and it offered a remarkable variety. During one weekend in January, for example, patrons could choose between seeing Laurence Olivier and Greer Garson in *Pride and Prejudice* at the Tivoli, Leslie Howard in *Pimpernel Smith* at the Central, Katharine Hepburn and Walter Huston in *Dragon Seed* at the Regal, Gary Cooper in *The Story of Dr Wassell* at the Victoria, Joel McCrea in *The Great Moment* at the Playhouse, Marlene Dietrich and John Wayne in *The Spoilers* at the Cosmopolitan, Ann Sheriden in *Angels Wash their Faces* at the Rex and Claude Dampier in *Such is Life* at the Kinema.

The improving weather helped the farmers. The January frosts had been very beneficial, especially on the heavy lands, and arrears of ploughing and planting had been made up. March was a "wonderful month", wrote a farmers' spokesman, with all seasonal work well forward despite labour shortage. Their only complaint was that the sugar beet factories at Bury St Edmunds and Ipswich had been closed prematurely, leaving hundreds of tons of beet in the fields and by the roadsides; the

Ministry for Agriculture argued that the sudden thaw had made the crop unfit for sugar manufacture.

As the prospect of an end to war in Europe drew closer, attitudes to the German people became a subject of lively debate in some quarters. Early in the year Sir Stafford Cripps, a Labour member of Churchill's government, suggested that when the post-war settlement was made, "We must not be revengeful or seek to advantage ourselves at the cost of others!" The leader-writer of the *East Anglian Daily Times* took up this theme:

> Hatred of evil, in whatever form, is needful, but it is doubtful, to say the least, if the British nation can include, to order, in the ambit of their hatred the millions of the Third Reich . . . The German people as a whole have a certain moral responsibility for the crimes of their leaders, but they are not themselves in the category of war criminals.

The opposite view was forcibly expressed by a Cambridge councillor, Captain A.C. Taylor. He was outraged by Cripps' attitude, called his sentiments "sloppy", and declared: "I believe the true opinion of the real English people is that Germany should be bombed and blasted, with all its inhabitants, off the face of the earth." The members of the Petersfield ward of the Cambridge Borough Conservative Association, to whom he addressed these remarks, clapped and cheered him. The local newspaper then published letters from a number of local residents who felt outraged by Captain Taylor's views, and some from those who agreed with him—such as a lady writing from Devonshire Road who asserted: "the more Germans exterminated, the better chance of peace in our time".

Two or three weeks later the army gave Captain Taylor an opportunity to visit the war front in Germany. When he returned he told Cambridge Rotarians how he had found Aachen: "Subjected to bombing and shell-fire, it has been fairly blotted out, and the results are simply terrifying. There was hardly a soul in its streets and the town was so blasted that it gave the visitor an eerie feeling." He failed to clarify whether this "terror" and "eerie feeling" had in any way caused an adjustment to his original views.

Official propagandists encouraged blanket condemnation of the Germans, arguing that the punishment being imposed upon them was a just retribution, and it was difficult for the regional press to resist this general mood. "Hun" was a conveniently short word for the headline-writers and much use was made of it, as in this example from the *Cambridge Evening News* front page on 17th January.

BRITISH NEAR HUN BORDER

The *East Anglian Daily Times,* however, bravely swam against the tide and regularly published photographs of bomb-wrecked German towns, homeless German refugees and other subjects that could have roused feelings of compassion.

As the Allied armies advanced into the German homeland, there were revelations that deeply affected and sometimes transformed public attitudes. They liberated camps in which men and women of many subjugated nations had been held as slave-labourers, and where there had been outbreaks of unbelievable ferocity.

When the US 3rd Army occupied Buchenwald, a camp four miles outside Weimar, they found records of the death there of 32,705 prisoners since its establishment in July 1937. They also found five hundred corpses piled up in a shed and twenty thousand survivors who were no more than living skeletons. The German SS guards left just before the Americans arrived, and the last thing they did was wreck the water system serving the camp. A few days later the British 11th Armoured Division occupied the Belsen camp, near Hanover, and found ten thousand unburied bodies, mostly of prisoners who had starved to death. After they had had time to investigate fully, they reported finding a total of thirty-five thousand corpses. A BBC correspondent, Richard Dimbleby, reported that the SS guards had shot two thousand inmates on the day before the British arrived. American troops who occupied a camp at Dachau were roused to such fury by what they saw that they summarily shot the German SS guards they confronted[9].

Few pictures of these horrors were printed in East Anglian newspapers, and mere words—whether in print or spoken on radio—could not convey much of the reality. Something of the evil was conveyed, however, by newsreel reports which were seen in the cinemas—though only in black and white—and on 20th April William Stock wrote in his diary: "Now we can really imagine what the German concentration camps were like. The sickening pictures prove that they were veritable slaughter-houses." After these films had been shown, there was a perceptible hardening of feeling against the Germans as a race. This was demonstrated by a dramatic change in the *East Anglian Daily Times'* editorial attitude. Its leading article on 16th April argued that the reports from the concentration camps had:

> surely stricken from our hearts whatever lingering belief there may have been that the German people could, by a policy of fraternisation and leniency, be brought within the pale of good neighbourliness. Not by that method will such characters be redeemed. Leopards do not change their spots that way . . . Germany, in a war of unprovoked aggression, has commited crimes without parallel; her people have displayed that with them the worship of violence remains, and that a cynical and callous contempt for decency in the treatment of humans is a cult.

In the last desperate weeks of the war many other horrors were reported from Germany. Hitler, from his underground bunker in Berlin, was ordering the summary execution of many high-ranking officers and officials whose loyalty, he feared, was suspect. Anyone who doubted or defied was dead. In this nightmare scenario many who had once been powerful committed suicide. Those who remained were brutalized. In Holland and Denmark the Germans were shooting many resistance leaders.

There was one execution in East Anglia, but by due process of law. A thirty-seven-year-old leading aircraftman from Lancashire who had been found guilty of murdering a WAAF in Beccles was hanged at Norwich Prison on 13th March. The ritual of execution demanded that certain dignitaries should attend as witnesses: the Under-Sheriff of Suffolk, a justice of the peace for the city of Norwich, the governor of the prison, the prison chaplain and the prison medical officer. At the inquest afterwards six of the seven Norfolk men who were called for jury service "expressed a wish to view the body", the *Eastern Daily Press* reported. They were under no obligation to do so; a free choice was offered to them. Had nearly six years of war begun, in some degree, to desensitize the men of Norfolk too?

When summer came the war in Europe was over. In East Anglia the feeling of relief was attenuated by the fact that thousands of local men remained prisoners-of-war in Japanese hands. Too much celebration would have seemed indecent; muted thanksgiving for partial deliverance was more appropriate. Nevertheless, there was gradual progress towards normality. June and July were hot and sunny. Harvesting began early, proceeded briskly and was completed by mid-September. Sailing began again on the Essex estuaries and on some of the Norfolk Broads. The coastal resorts were crowded at weekends. There was a new government in power to underline the idea of a fresh start.

'The Squander Bug' was devised as part of the National Savings campaign. *Eastern Daily Press*

Shortages of many goods persisted and the need for conservation was constantly emphasized. There was continued emphasis on saving—small investors in the eastern counties had already saved more than two hundred million pounds during the five war years. This campaign now featured an evil "Squander Bug". Newsprint was still strictly rationed so that readers had only mini-newspapers. Throughout the year Norfolk's leading newspaper, the *Eastern Daily Press*, published six-page issues only twice a week; on other days the paper was a single folded sheet.

At the height of summer Japan faced its atomic nemesis and surrendered unconditionally. The men of the Royal Norfolk, Suffolk and Cambridgeshire Regiments who had survived the harsh conditions of the Far Eastern prison camps were liberated at last. The thoughts of every East Anglian family turned to demobilization and the prospect of an early return of menfolk. In many homes there were exchanges such as the following:

"Daddy will be home soon, I hope."

"Mummy, what's Daddy like?"

"He's very nice, darling. You'll love him."

"But, Mummy, what does he look like?"

There were many cases where children ranging up to four years of age and their fathers had never met.

Autumn unfolded into winter, a chill returned to the air, and harsh realities pressed in upon the people. Even the reunion of families was not always easy. Problems were sufficiently widespread for the *East Anglian Daily Times* to publish a leading article on the matter, asserting:

> Now that homecomings are of daily occurrence, in many instances the reality is proving woefully unlike the picture painted in advance by mingled memories and anticipation. Disappointment and despair are felt also by not a few wives . . . Marriage vows have been held in light regard or temporarily forgotten under the stress of prolonged separation. Suspicions darken the reunion; infidelities are admitted on the part of husband or wife, sometimes of both.

Pointing out that many couples were without homes of their own in which they could settle, the article urged that they be treated charitably.

The Bishop of Norwich also spoke on the subject:

> The homes have been the biggest war casualty. Evacuation, air raids, service of men and women in the forces, the factories and the fields, a decay of home discipline and preoccupation with wartime difficulties of food, clothing and so on, have produced an evil crop of broken marriages, juvenile crime and sexual immorality . . .

There were, of course, many homes to which the menfolk did not return. Some endured an agonizing wait because weeks passed before it was known whether individual servicemen had survived. Either they turned up or they did not. Serious as were such problems, they affected only a minority. More usually there was unalloyed joy at reunion, and gratitude for having been spared.

This gratitude found expression in the churches and also in other practical ways. After the liberation of the Netherlands about fifty thousand Dutch children suffering from near-starvation were brought to Britain. After spending two months in hostels for gradual and careful adjustment of their diet, they stayed for a further two months as guests of families living in the country.

In Norwich the Lord Mayor presided over a hospitality committee that accepted five hundred children, aged ten to fifteen. Half of them arrived in October and the other half in November, in groups of twenty, each with a leader. They were met by Red Cross and Women's Voluntary Service ladies and taken to Boulton and Paul's premises to be medically examined and given tea. None spoke English, so they hailed the Lord Mayor by singing "For he's a jolly good fellow" in Dutch and followed this up with both the Dutch and the British national anthems. Over a hundred of the children stayed with Norwich families and the rest went to Aylsham, Brundall, Cantley, Coltishall, Dereham, Diss, Downham Market, Fakenham, Harleston, Holt, Hunstanton, King's Lynn, Loddon, North Walsham, Shotesham, Swaffham, Thetford, Watton, Wells and Wymondham. Many of the visitors attended local schools.

This generous hospitality was offered against a background of continuing uncertainty about Britain's own food supplies. With the end of the war Lend-Lease shipments from the United States were cut off, and by September Britain faced the urgent problem of feeding and clothing her population during the coming winter. Emissaries went to Washington to discuss the matter, and on 17th September President Truman announced: "The US government is now in a position to fulfil the main requests of Europe—with the exception of sugar, fats and oils—from this date until January . . .".

The dockers working in the biggest British ports then took a hand. In October they staged a strike which was reported in these front-page headlines in the *Eastern Daily Press*:

BREAD MAY HAVE TO BE RATIONED

Docks strike effect on wheat ships

Home acreage has decreased

Not even during the darkest days of the war had bread been rationed. In the event the strike was settled and rationing averted, and British farmers were urged on to another supreme effort of food production in the year ahead.

Such was the flavour of the year that is reviewed in the following pages. For most people it was both sweet and sour. As it ended even the most optimistic of men and women understood that the peace that had been won would bring no easy years of plenty and prosperity. The horror and despair had been banished; the best that remained was hope.

CHAPTER TWO

Transformation of the Bombers

ON 24th APRIL 1945 something like a miracle occurred on air bases throughout East Anglia. Bombers which for years had been delivering death-dealing cargoes to cities and towns all over the European Continent were suddenly transformed into carriers of life-saving food and medicines. The transformation was effected in a matter of twenty-four hours—though it had been long prepared.

The plight of the starving Dutch had concerned the Allied authorities from the moment that the end of hostilities came into sight. Early in 1945 a Lancaster and crew from Witchford had been sent to Netheravon to conduct trials, dropping bags of food from low level. Practice drops were demonstrated to VIPs on 6th April. The Allies then arranged with the Germans through neutral sources for relief to be sent. Lancasters flew on these mercy missions from Mepal, Waterbeach, Witchford and Wratting Common; and USAAF Flying Fortresses and Liberators flew from Eye, Framlingham, Knettishall, Mendlesham, Snetterton Heath and Wendling.

The Dutch marked the ground with a white cross with a red light in the middle and a green circle of light around. Notwithstanding the careful rehearsals, when the first actual drop took place—at two airfields and a race track at The Hague and on an open space near Rotterdam—many of the sacks burst on impact. The problem was solved, and between 29th April and 7th May Bomber Command, each Lancaster carrying five packs of provisions, delivered 6,672 tons of food before the German surrender at the end of the war allowed ships and road transport to enter the area. The Dutch painted huge white letters on rooftops, appealing for sweets for children and for tobacco, and the airmen obliged.

This was but one part of a last flurry of humanitarian activity on British and American bases before they were finally closed. Fortresses from Rougham carried out widespread leaflet-dropping, mainly to assist displaced persons. Several bases found themselves ferrying thousands of men and women around Europe. Fortresses at Snetterton Heath moved personnel to Morocco, France, Germany and Ireland; and Liberators at Eye flew other refugees and troops back to their home countries. An RAF squadron at Tuddenham took part in Operation Dodge, flying Italian prisoners home to Italy; and a Rivenhall RAF Transport squadron helped carry an occupation force to Norway.

There were 166,000 Commonwealth prisoners-of-war alive in Germany when the war ended[1]. Bomber Command Stirlings and Lancasters flew to Brussels, and later to other airfields, to bring them home. Priority was given to the

Loading food into a Lancaster at Wratting Common to be dropped at The Hague. *Haverhill Echo*

wounded and sick, and one hundred ex-prisoners-of-war arrived in Cambridge from Germany on 25th April and went into wards in Addenbrookes, the Leys Annexe and the Examination Hall. Another 140 followed a week later.

On a single day—8th May—more than thirteen thousand ex-prisoners were flown from Europe to Britain. Squadrons from Rivenhall, Tuddenham, Waterbeach, Witchford and Wratting Common took part, as well as American bombers from Eye and Glatton. Nearly four thousand Indian ex-prisoners-of-war were assembled at Mundford, where the King and Queen visited them on 16th June.

Once the ex-prisoners had been repatriated many RAF bases in East Anglia prepared for closure. Within weeks the planes had left eleven of the 3 Group fields: Alconbury, Bourn, Downham Market, East Wretham, Foulsham, Lakenheath, Little Snoring, Marham, Newmarket, Woolfox Lodge and Wyton. Some bases found new peacetime roles. Several among them—including Debach, Rivenhall and Wratting Common—became camps for displaced persons who had no homes in Europe to which to return.

At first Rivenhall handled servicemen coming home on leave or to be demobilized; customs facilities were installed and it became one of the busiest airfields in East Anglia. Later it settled down to daily trips to Brussels, Munster and Schleswig: and occasional trips to Copenhagen, Prague and Vienna, taking mail and newspapers to the Army of Occupation and relief supplies to the people of the occupied countries. Towards the end of 1945 the disused Rivenhall buildings were turned into "The Polish Camp" and Polish Army personnel released from prison camps formed a strong community there*[2].

These missions of mercy were preceded by a relentless bombing assault on Germany, marking the final phase of the titanic struggle begun in September 1939. In the course of four months more damage was done to the German homeland by explosives loaded at bomber bases in East Anglia than by all the artillery massed by the armies at the fighting fronts.

The bases were thick on the ground. The RAF had three of its eight groups comprising Bomber Command in East Anglia. No 3 Group, fully equipped with the most modern Lancaster bombers, occupied more than a score of airfields within a triangle defined by Alconbury in the west, Chedburgh in the east and Foulsham in the north. No 8 Group, the "Pathfinder" Force, straddled the Cambridgeshire–Huntingdonshire border, with Lancaster Squadrons at Downham Market, Oakington, Upwood and Warboys, and Mosquito Squadrons at five other airfields. No 100 Group was at four airfields in north Norfolk; its Mosquitos did not carry bombs but a variety of electronic appliances to jam German radar and radio signals from ground controllers. The Bomber Command Headquarters was at High Wycombe. The bombing force was supported by RAF fighters and fighter-bombers flying from more than a dozen bases in the region.

Powerful as this British armada was, it was outnumbered in East Anglia by the units of the USAAF, whose 8th Air Force consisted of two hundred thousand men and more than 2,400 bombers and 1,200 fighters, operating from sixty airfields—most of them in the area between Peterborough and the North Sea.

Every day the people of the eastern counties watched an almost non-stop stream of warplanes flying away over the horizon; they saw them as evidence of a single-minded and resolute policy of attack. The fact was that the war chiefs were bitterly divided and the Chief of RAF Bomber Command was close to losing his job. Seeds of discord had been planted long before, for RAF and USAAF bombing strategies had never been fully in accord. From 1942 the British had opted for large-area targets, attempting night-time "saturation bombing" of German cities with the aim of destroying factories and undermining morale. The Americans from their first arrival in Britain had attempted precision bombing from a high level during daylight of carefully selected industrial and economic targets.

Air Chief Marshal Sir Arthur Harris, Chief of Bomber Command, was a determined advocate of area bombing. During 1943 he had directed a series of

*Later they were joined by their families and other demobbed Polish servicemen. Many married local girls and became integrated. Some emigrated to the colonies with government assistance, and some returned to Poland. It was closed down in the mid nineteen-fifties.

assaults on the cities of the Ruhr, on Hamburg and on Berlin. When RAF losses in these raids mounted alarmingly and criticism of the policy began to be voiced, Harris responded vigorously. He assured the Air Ministry in December 1943 that his force of Lancasters alone would be able to destroy between forty and fifty per cent of the principal German towns and that this would "produce in Germany by 1st April 1944 a state of devastation in which surrender is inevitable"[3]. Others argued differently.

For nearly six months before and after the D-Day invasion of Normandy Harris lost his power to influence bombing policy as control of all air forces passed to Eisenhower, the Supreme Commander. Because the invasion involved concentrated bombing of specific railway and transport targets to deny the German defenders their lines of communication and supply, the "saturation" raids were abandoned for a period. Harris did not waver in his attitude; he fought doggedly against diverting his planes to give direct assistance to the troops landing in Normandy[4]. Later, when the British and US armies were advancing towards the German frontier in November 1944, Harris declared that if Bomber Command were allowed to destroy the fifteen "principal industrial centres of population" in Germany to which it had not yet given attention "it will do more towards accelerating the defeat of Germany than the armies have yet done—or will do"[5].

When Eisenhower's direct control of the bombers ended in September 1944, the Air Ministry identified specific targets the destruction of which—according to the government's economic advisers—would destroy Germany's capacity for war. These targets were factories producing molybdenum and ball-bearings, oil installations and communications. Harris was instructed that Bomber Command should make the area attacks he preferred only "when weather or tactical conditions are unsuitable for operations against specific primary objectives"[6]. Harris did not conceal his scorn of the economic experts, and only six per cent of Bomber Command's total effort in October was directed against oil plants—about half the scale of the effort made between June and September—while more than twice the weight of bombs was dropped on German cities than in any previous month[7].

The year 1944 ended with Sir Charles Portal, Chief of Air Staff, telling Harris he was "profoundly disappointed" and adding: "It is difficult to feel that your staff can be devoting its maximum thought and energies to the accomplishment of your first priority task if you yourself are not wholeheartedly in support of it."

Harris responded indignantly:

> I do not give my staff views, I give them orders . . . I have told them to miss no opportunity of prosecuting the oil plan and they have missed no worthwhile opportunity. But that does not relieve me of my duty to inform you that like all previous panaceas so enthusiastically put forward by the Ministry of Economic Warfare the basis of the plan is wrong[8].

The row thus reached a climax as 1945 began. The Air Staff had decided on one policy; the head of Bomber Command wanted another. On 18th January Harris offered to resign[9]. Portal and the Air Minister then backed down, Portal writing: "I willingly accept your assurance that you will continue to do your utmost to ensure the successful execution of the policy laid down. I am very sorry that you do not believe in it."[10]

While these differences at high level were being resolved, snow, frost and fog combined to curtail flying activity during January and much of February. The assault on oil installations—including targets in eastern Europe—and on German communications continued sporadically. Harris still devoted as much effort as possible to a general attack on German cities—"area bombing"—and German towns near the battle fronts were steadily reduced to ruins. RAF and USAAF bombers from East Anglian bases took part in every big raid.

The US 381st Bomb Group at Ridgewell, for example, joined raids on targets in Germany on fourteen nights during January. Returning from one of these missions, two Flying Fortresses collided in mid-air while circling the base and eighteen men were killed. RAF Lancasters from 3 and 8 Groups were involved in a major assault on Nuremburg on 2nd/3rd January, when a total force of 514 Lancasters and seven Mosquitos destroyed the centre of that city. Industrial and railway areas were severely damaged as was intended, and the castle, the *rathaus*, almost all the churches and about two thousand preserved medieval houses also went up in flames. The death toll was put at 1,838, with at least fifty more missing[11].

Clearing frost from the rear-gunner's window of a B17 of the USAAF 91st Bomb Group at Bassingbourne, January 1945.   *Imperial War Museum*

Cambridge Daily News

Another big raid some time afterwards was on Wiesbaden and carried out by over five hundred RAF bombers. The town's important war industries along the riverside were untouched, but approximately one thousand people were killed and 350 injured[12]. A day later the US 8th Air Force hit Berlin, putting more planes into the air than on any other day during the war apart from D-Day. They spread out for three hundred miles. The Commanding Officer at Ridgewell went up in a non-combat plane to watch the force assembling over Suffolk. He flew well above them, and the chaplain—who was with him—described what they saw:

> Bombers were in the air as far as the eye could see, ahead of us and back of us, Group after Group, Wing after Wing, until the entire First Division of the Eighth Air Force was assembled. I knew that they were out to destroy Berlin . . .[13]

They succeeded. The Allied air forces now had mastery of the skies over Germany, and it was there that most of their efforts were directed. Sometimes there was a diversion, as when a force of Lancasters of RAF 8 Group took off from East Anglian bases during January to join what became a highly controversial raid on the French town of Royan, at the mouth of the Gironde. Most of France was in Allied hands, but a German garrison was holding out stubbornly in Royan, preventing the Allies from using the port of Bordeaux. In a two-wave attack the RAF destroyed four-fifths of the town and killed many hundreds—perhaps as many as eight hundred—French civilians, but only thirty-five to fifty Germans. There were bitter recriminations and an American air force officer involved in the decision to mount the raid was removed from his command. The German garrison did not surrender until fifteen weeks later[14].

The controversy over this raid was mild, however, compared to that which developed after RAF and USAAF bombers attacked the east German city of Dresden on 13 and 14th February.

After careful consideration at the highest level—which included consultation with Sir Arthur Harris and reference to the Prime Minister—it was decided during January that the RAF would make all-out attacks more or less simultaneously on Berlin, Breslau, Munich, Chemnitz, Leipzig and Dresden[15]. These cities all lay just behind the German lines on the eastern front and they were packed with German refugees and wounded from areas recently captured by the Red Army. The directive given to Bomber Command by the Air Ministry on 27th January stated that the attacks had "the particular object of exploiting the confused conditions which are likely to exist in the above-mentioned cities during the successful Russian advance"[16]. The decision had effectively been taken before the conference of the British, American and Soviet leaders at Yalta, at which the Russians requested British and US air support in the east; but that request was later cited as the reason for what were described as "attacks on the German army's lines of communication in the Berlin–Dresden–Leipzig region"[17].

The date of the raid on Dresden was decided by the US 8th Air Force, which was to make the first attack, but this was cancelled because of weather conditions. In the event only the Pathfinder Force of No 3 Group took off from East Anglian bases; three other RAF groups flew from Lincolnshire and Yorkshire. They made two separate raids three hours apart during the night of 13th/14th February. In the first 244 Lancasters took part, and in the second 529 Lancasters. The following day the USAAF sent 311 B-17s to make a follow-up attack. They also sent Mustang fighter-bombers:

> Mustangs, with no enemy fighters to engage, swept over the city machine-gunning anything that moved, including the lorries of the relief organisations now converging on Dresden, and groups of bombed-out people lining the banks of the Elbe or thronging the Grosser Garten park, an assembly point for bombed-out children.[18]

The RAF assault on Dresden did not feature prominently in the war reports in the East Anglian newspapers. The *Cambridge Daily News,* for example, made it the third story on its front page, with only a single column heading:

CRIMEA TALKS IN ACTION: R.A.F. – U.S. BLOWS AT DRESDEN

300 miles stream of bombers

The *East Anglian Daily Times* gave a clearer indication of the results of the raids, with a top-of-column front-page story headed:

DRESDEN ROCKED BY DOUBLE AIR BLOW

650,000 fire bombs on city.

Later, however, most newspapers quoted a German radio broadcast reporting:

the greatest destruction a big urban area has ever suffered. In the inner town not a single block of buildings, not a single detached building, remains intact, or even capable of reconstruction. The town area is devoid of human life. A great city has been wiped from the map of Europe. Tens of thousands who lived in the city are now buried under its ruins. Even an attempt at identification of the victims is hopeless ... There were one million people in Dresden, including 600,000 bombed-out evacuees and refugees from the east. The raging fires which spread irresistibly in the narrow streets killed a great many from sheer lack of oxygen ...

The official British response to this account was ambivalent; should it be used as evidence of the success of Bomber Command, or should it be dismissed as enemy propaganda suggesting genocide? There was no question but that the RAF had created a firestorm in which large areas of the city were burnt out, but no one could know how many people had died. Informed guesses put the figure at "over 50,000"*.

Many people expressed unease. In East Anglia public debate centred around Richard R. Stokes, the Member of Parliament for Ipswich, who had frequently protested in the House of Commons against earlier "saturation" bombing of German cities. Now he raised the matter of the Dresden raid during a parliamentary debate on the air estimates on 6th March. "There is no case whatever, under any conditions, in my view, for terror bombing", he said. The Under-Secretary for Air replied: "We are not wasting bombers or time on purely terror tactics . . .".

Public controversy persisted but the government stood its ground. Behind the scenes, however, war leaders of the highest rank were seriously at odds. On 28th March Churchill sent a Minute to his chiefs of staff:

It seems to me that the moment has come when the question of bombing German cities simply for the sake of increasing the terror, though under other pretexts, should be reviewed. Otherwise we shall come into control of an utterly ruined land. The destruction of Dresden remains a serious query against the conduct of Allied bombing ... I feel the need for more precise concentration upon military objectives, such as oil and communications behind the immediate battle-zone, rather than on mere acts of terror and wanton destruction, however impressive.[20]

When these comments were passed to Bomber Command, its chief, Sir Arthur Harris, was predictably irate. Within hours he replied that reference to "terror and wanton destruction" were:

an insult both to the bombing policy of the Air Ministry and to the manner in which that policy had been executed by Bomber Command ... We have never gone in for terror bombing ... Attacks on cities, like any other act of war, are intolerable unless they are strategically justified. But they are strategically justified in so far as they tend to shorten the war and so preserve the lives of Allied soldiers ... I do not personally regard the whole of the remaining cities of Germany as worth the bones of the one British Grenadier . . .[21]

---

*According to Longmate[19] the best post-war estimate was that 135,000 died in Dresden, but to this day no one really knows.

Once again, as in January, Harris forced his critics into retreat. Churchill withdrew his Minute and substituted a much milder one on 1st April:

It seems to me the moment when the question of the so-called "area-bombing" of German cities should be reviewed from the point of view of our own interests. If we come into control of an entirely ruined land, there will be a great shortage of accommodation for ourselves and our allies.[22]

In other raids during February many industrial targets were destroyed. An important synthetic oil plant at Politz was so damaged that it produced no more oil during the war. A very accurate raid on Essen placed three hundred high explosive bombs and eleven thousand incendiaries on the Krupps works.

But also during February enormous damage was done to several historic German towns. The RAF destroyed about forty per cent of the built-up area of Worms, including the cathedral and most of the churches and cultural buildings in the old town. Of its population of 58,000, 35,000 lost their homes. At Pforzheim an area measuring three kilometres by one-and-a-half was completely engulfed in

The industrial area of an unidentified German town, left in ruins after Allied air raids.

Photo courtesy of Ian Hawkins

French civilians and American soldiers around a B17 of the 569th Bombardment Squadron, 390th Bomb Group, based at Framlingham, which crash-landed near Steinburg, France, on 20th January during a mission to marshalling yards at Heilbronn, Germany. The crew baled out and the pilot brought the aircraft in, receiving only minor injuries.   *D. Glover*

flames. Over four-fifths of the town's built-up area was destroyed—"probably the greatest proportion in one raid during the war". In this city the death toll was put at 17,600. In Mainz 5,670 buildings were destroyed, including most of the historic old town, and at least 1,122 were killed[23].

The US 8th Air Force meanwhile spent the last few days of February and the first three of March flying one thousand planes in support of "Operation Clarion"—an all-out assault on German communication centres. They flew at six thousand to ten thousand feet in an attempt, they said, to reduce civilian casualties as well as to achieve greater accuracy.

The war was clearly reaching its climax. Allied armies had crossed the German frontier at a number of points and Montgomery was preparing for the 21st Army's assault on the Rhine. The RAF became busy by night with close-support bombing just behind the German front line.

On many of the East Anglian bases preparations were made from mid-February for "Operation Varsity", by which the RAF and the USAAF were to assist the Rhine crossing. The daily sight of Stirling "tugs" towing Horsa gliders on long training flights led civilians in the eastern counties to make an informed guess that the final assault on Germany was imminent. Nevertheless elaborate security measures were taken. At Woodbridge the base was sealed off for five days while gliders were assembled, and similar restrictions were imposed at other airfields including Rivenhall, Earls Colne and Gosfield: no one was allowed to leave, post a letter or use the telephone.

When the time came the gliders landed troops on the east bank of the river Rhine. Planes from Rivenhall had the distinction of leading the airborne fleet. Aircrews and glider pilots were called at 2 am on 24th March and given a final briefing, and then troops and equipment were loaded into the Horsas, which had been assembled in a tight group at the end of the runway. Sixty Stirling "tugs" were lined up along the perimeter track. One by one they moved on to the runway, and one by one the gliders were hauled forward by tractor and tow ropes were attached. The first pair took off at 7 am and as each cleared the end of the runway the next was given the signal to go. They made a rendezvous over Kent with other groups, until altogether there were 1,696 transport planes and 1,348 gliders (some in double tow) carrying 21,680 troops, with 889 fighters acting as escort.

The USAAF took an American airborne division to the Rhine, some paratroops in giant C-47 transport planes from Wethersfield and other troops in gliders from other bases. At the USAAF base at Ridgewell in Essex, James Good Brown watched the planes on their way:

> At the break of dawn, I saw something phenomenal: gliders trailing behind troop transport ships . . . hundreds of planes with their gliders attached came passing before our sight. They came and they went. Not high up, just above the treetops. I stood for one hour at the window of the tower watching. I knew that THE PUSH WAS ON.[24]

The assault force flew to its target in spring sunshine. It was a perfect day with no cloud in the sky. After a five-hour flight the Stirlings returned to East Anglia in time for lunch.

Meanwhile thousands of other aircraft, British and American, ensured that the Luftwaffe did not interfere with the landings, blasting German defences near the Rhine and airfields, bridges and marshalling yards further back. Brown also noted in his diary how this operation looked from Ridgewell.

> The 381st put their 50 Flying Fortresses into the air for their two raids on this day. As I watched our planes rising one at a time to gain altitude, I saw an entire group of heavies from another base already assembled. From the lead ships in the darkness came flares of all colors. The sky looked like the Fourth of July back home. Now our leader from the 381st was in the air, and he was shooting his particular color for identification. In half an hour we saw an unusual sight—a whole group of shining silver ships glistening in the sunlight. It was dark on the earth. Upstairs it was light. The bend of the earth's surface permitted the sun to shine on the ships and not on us. Each plane sparkled with the brilliance of a diamond in the sky.[25]

Once Montgomery's troops had crossed the Rhine the USAAF helped keep them supplied: 240 Liberators dropped medical supplies, food and weapons to them from an altitude of fifty feet.

By the end of March the bombers' task in the European war was almost done. There was a crescendo of activity during the month. Berlin was bombed regularly.

On 15th March the entire US 8th Air Force[26] raided the German High Command headquarters at Zossen, near Berlin. The RAF dropped 67,637 tons—the greatest weight of bombs in any month of the war. Oil targets deep in eastern Germany were hit, towns near the battle front were reduced to ruins, and some German cities were selected for the first time as new targets. Lancasters from 3 Group stations in East Anglia engaged in big raids on Cologne, Essen and Dortmund. The American troops who entered Cologne a few days after one of these raids cleared at least four hundred bodies from the streets. Most of Essen was already in ruins after earlier raids. Then 1,108 planes which bombed Dortmund were the biggest force ever sent to one target during the war. Other big RAF raids were on Wurzburg, where ninety per cent of the built-up area was destroyed and estimates of the dead varied from four thousand to five thousand; on Hanau, where all churches, hospitals, schools and historic buildings in the old town were badly damaged and approximately two thousand were killed; and on Hildesheim, where seventy per cent of the town was destroyed—including the cathedral, most of the churches and many other historic buildings—and 1,645 were thought to have died[27].

The Allied superiority in the air was overwhelming and these raids were made with minimal loss. The Germans' reporting system had broken down so that they were unable to compile reliable records of damage and casualties. Their cities were virtually paralysed until the Allied troops occupied them later[28]. The final USAAF mission of the war was to bomb four rail complexes surrounding Berchtesgaden, while 315 RAF Lancasters simultaneously bombed Hitler's "Eagle Nest" retreat there.

The last weeks of the air war were not without misadventure of various kinds. The USAAF suffered a series of accidents in January. One of its bombers crashed and caused a great deal of damage on the outskirts of Bury St Edmunds: most of its crew were killed. Eight days later two Flying Fortresses collided in mid-air and came down at Tilbury-juxta-Clare in Essex, where they went up in flames near the Fox public house, killing all their crews. Eight days after that two more Fortresses collided above the Duke of Norfolk's estate and crashed in flames, scattering bombs and debris over a wide area. Again the crews of both planes died. Most of the bombs fell near the village street at North Lopham which had to be closed for a couple of days, and many windows were smashed.

A US bomber pilot returning to Wendling in March flew over the field firing flares to celebrate his final mission—a prevalent practice, but one which was strictly forbidden because it endangered aircrews and men on the ground. On this occasion the Liberator caught fire and crashed from two thousand feet. The pilot and seven of his crew died[29].

An embarrassing episode occurred when US planes bombed neutral Switzerland. Part of a force of twenty-eight B-24s from Attlebridge—whose mission to a designated German target was aborted because of cloud—dropped their bombs instead on what they thought was Frieburg in the Black Forest. In fact they hit the centre of Basle, mainly around the main railway station, and to compound the offence they machine-gunned a train. Four people died. Other US planes unintentionally bombed Zurich. General Spaatz secretly visited Switzerland to explain and apologize, and many millions of dollars were paid to the Swiss government as reparation[30].

There was a bizarre incident in the final weeks of the war when an RAF gunner fell through the floor of the bomb bay of his Halifax after it had been damaged during a raid. His parachute harness caught on the fuselage and he was left dangling. He hung thus for three-and-a-half hours while the plane struggled back to Britain. The pilot put down at Woodbridge, one of three airfields which had been built specifically to take aircraft returning damaged or short of fuel. The gunner's oxygen mask and goggles scraped the runway as the plane landed, but he survived unhurt.

Even when the war in Europe had ended, air force men still died. On 12th May two bombers crashed in East Anglia: an RAF plane demolished the YMCA at Langham and a B-17 crashed on the outskirts of Diss. In each case one man was killed and other crew members were injured.

After victory in Europe many bomber squadrons were earmarked for the Far East to continue the war against Japan. At Stradishall RAF planes were painted white in preparation but, as we shall see, the Japanese surrendered before most units could be moved[31].

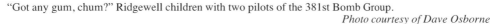

"Got any gum, chum?" Ridgewell children with two pilots of the 381st Bomb Group.
Photo courtesy of Dave Osborne

CHAPTER THREE

Victory in Europe

THE LAST four months of the war were a continuation of that phase which had begun with the break-out from Normandy. A German offensive in the Ardennes at the end of 1944 had been a shock and had caused a major redistribution of Allied forces in Luxembourg, Belgium and Holland, upsetting their time-table for an advance to the Rhine. The Germans had failed, however, in their effort to recapture Brussels and Antwerp; by late January they were driven out of the Ardennes and the front was stabilized. On other war fronts there had been disappointments. In the east the Russians had made little advance since the summer of 1944, and much of Poland remained in German occupation. A new Russian offensive was launched on 12th January. The Red Army burst through German defences north and south of Warsaw, in six days crossed the German frontier and advanced into the industrial zone of Silesia, and by the end of the month was only forty-five miles from Berlin. In Italy the Allies had failed to break out of the mountains into the Po valley and seemed unlikely to do so before the spring. None the less when Churchill reviewed the war situation in the Commons on 18th January he promised that henceforth the whole eastern and western fronts, and that in Italy, would be kept in constant flame until the final climax was reached.

The Germans still occupied north and west Holland. The Allied front extended from Nijmegen in the north, along the Maas, east of the Ardennes and Luxembourg and the Saar, and into Alsace. As 1945 began Allied efforts were directed towards crossing the rivers, which were preliminary obstacles before the Rhine. Several battalions from the eastern counties were to play a major role in the campaign.

The 3rd division of Montgomery's Army held the line on the river Maas. For much of January the snow lay deep and men shivered in the trenches and patrolled in white camouflage suits; on 10th January twenty-seven degrees of frost were recorded. The 1st Battalion of the Suffolks and the 1st Battalion of the Royal Norfolks were part of this force. The Suffolks (part of 8 Brigade) had been there since December and remained until the first week of February. It was fairly quiet during most of this time, but there was a period early in January when the battalion was heavily shelled. Standing patrols were maintained along the river at night and occasional enemy reconnaissance patrols which crossed were engaged and driven off.

The 1st Royal Norfolks (part of 185 Brigade) moved up on 6th January to an area of the Maas line in the vicinity of Meerlo. The Germans held a small bridgehead over the river in a wood on the battalion's left flank, but this was eliminated a couple of days later by a company of the 1st Suffolks in armoured troop carriers. The Norfolks remained on the river line for the remainder of January, patrolling, wiring and digging. An *Eastern Daily Press* correspondent visited them and reported:

> For the forward companies life is entirely in dugouts, and at one place in open trenches, which they man in turn on a rota system . . . As I arrived at the dugouts Major Bagwell and his men had just returned from a patrol wearing their newly-issued snow suits. It was much like a scene from the Russian front. Underground, men were grouped around oil stoves and making themselves foot protection which someone has dubbed "Robinson Crusoe" shoes — sandbags filled with straw in which the lads move over the snow-covered fields with the elegance of elephants.

Away from the front line, however, there were:

> some men of the battalion [who] have taken up serious study in the difficult conditions of active service. One of them hopes to qualify for the teaching profession. At battalion headquarters I was shown applications from other Norfolk men for courses in agriculture, higher mathematics, organic chemistry and journalism, books being supplied to them through Army Education Corps channels.

When the Norfolks were given leave, many of them went back to Helmond, a Dutch town about twenty miles behind the front. They had received a fantastic reception there when they had liberated it in 1944, and many families remained anxious to be their hosts. The *Eastern Daily Press* reporter found:

> most of the local inhabitants speaking English as a result, not without a Norfolk flavour . . . The Norfolk badge [is] Helmond's most popular brooch design and I have seen here Dutch girls sporting Royal Norfolk Regiment flashes on the sleeves of their coats.

There were Essex men, too, on this northern sector of the front. The 2nd Battalion of the Essex Regiment was part of the 1st Canadian Army, which began 1945 in an area near Nijmegen which the Germans had flooded by destroying the dykes. It was a no-man's-land (and water) which they patrolled in boats, or by wading through frosty water or skating over crunchy ice.

In the third week of January the Germans attacked towards Nijmegen from the north, aiming to secure the bridge there. They occupied the small town of Zetten and the Essex men were ordered to recapture it. The attack was made astride the main road where the snow lay several inches deep, because the country on either side of it was flooded or intersected every few yards by ditches that were insufficiently frozen to carry a man's weight. There was extremely tough fighting: "every room, cellar and outhouse had to be cleared in fierce close fighting . . . a slow and costly business"[1]. The centre of the town was reached at 1.30 pm on the first day, after four hours of room-to-room combat, and the battle continued without respite until the whole town was finally taken before first light the next

The 2nd Essex battalion in Zetten, 22nd January, 1945.   *Photo courtesy of Col. T. A. Martin*

morning. Eight Essex men were killed and fifty-two wounded, but the enemy lost about seven hundred—387 of them taken prisoner, the others killed or wounded.

The Essex battalion then returned to Nijmegen, resumed an interrupted rest period, and by 25th January was within one hundred to four hundred yards of the German front line, in a sector around the village of Haalderen with the Waal just on their right, flowing well above ground level within its dykes. Every house in this area was damaged, most had been fortified with sandbags and banked earth, and the few that were not defended had been mined. The whole area was constantly swept by enemy fire so that, notwithstanding their white camouflage suits, the Essex men were unable to move about during daylight. As January ended a rapid thaw caused the Maas to flood and much of the surrounding countryside was inundated, many roads became impassable and mud stopped offensive operations.

Early in February Suffolk and Norfolk men moved back from the front line. The Suffolk battalion went to Haacht, a small Belgian town not far from Brussels, where the men were billeted in civilian houses for sixteen days. This was their pleasantest fortnight between D-Day and VE-Day, even though part of it was spent training in river crossing and street fighting. The 1st Norfolks spent three weeks

Men of 14 Platoon, C Company, 1st Royal Norfolk Regiment at Mierlo, Holland on 27th January, rehearsing for the crossing of the River Maas.   *Imperial War Museum*

near Maastricht, where battalion officers produced a complete operation order and staff tables for an assault across a major river obstacle. This involved much practice work, so that everyone was kept busy. The plan, in its entirety, was used for the initial crossing of the Rhine on 23rd March, although the Royal Norfolks themselves were not immediately involved[2].

On 8th February Montgomery announced a new British and Canadian offensive: the big push forward from the river Maas, over the German frontier and up to the west bank of the Rhine. From Nijmegen a road ran south-eastward, roughly parallel to and only a few miles from the Rhine, passing through the towns of Kleve, Kalkar and Xanten. Between this road and the Rhine the Allied armour was concentrated in preparation for the assault on the river barrier. South of Xanten, in a loop of the river opposite Wesel, pockets of German troops remained to be dealt with.

During the first three days of the offensive Montgomery's troops advanced ten miles and took the first major German town, Kleve. They then encountered strong enemy resistance, mud and flood. Bitter temperatures made things more difficult, and it was 21st February before they captured the German strongpoint of Goch.

31

The advance was then resumed. At this point the 3rd Division—including the 1st Suffolk and 1st Royal Norfolk Battalions—moved out of the Netherlands in long convoys of lorries, tracked vehicles, gun-tractors and trailers; crossed the river Maas on a long Bailey bridge to the village of Gennep; and came in three or four miles to the German frontier. They were unlikely to forget their first impression of the enemy homeland. As one recalled afterwards.

> Through complete devastation the Division made its way until the sound of guns reached their ears. At a distance it was a continuous reverberation, and as they approached the rubble that was heaped on the site of the town of Goch they came right in amongst the perpetual bang and crack of the gun-areas.[3]

Some battalions of 8 Brigade, of which the 1st Suffolk was part, soon suffered heavy casualties and as a result the brigade was moved into divisional reserve. The 1st Battalion of the Royal Norfolks, part of 185 Brigade, advanced to Pfalzdorf near Goch. The remainder of the division took up positions facing the small town of Kervenheim, which was the pivot of the German defensive positions and was very strongly held by the 7th Parachute Regiment. The country in front of the British was low lying and boggy with many small woods beyond which, on the other side of a small ridge, lay the Rhine.

On 1st March 185 Brigade was ordered to capture Kervenheim. A heavy artillery barrage was laid down before the advance began, and then—while two other battalions secured the flanks—the Norfolks passed through to assault the town, supported by a squadron of tanks. This proved to be one of the battalion's most costly engagements of the war. The Germans maintained heavy fire and drove back several initial efforts, but eventually the Norfolks gained a footing at the edge of the town and two companies of the 2nd Battalion of the Lincolns came up to help them consolidate. After holding their ground through the night, next morning they found that the Germans had withdrawn. Forty-one Norfolk men were killed and 120 wounded, with four others missing; three officers were awarded the Military Cross.

A great concentration of Allied artillery, tanks, vehicles and infantry was now assembled between the road and the Rhine. North of the 3rd Division the Canadians were fighting towards Uedem. To the south the 53rd Division was advancing slowly towards Geldern against stiff opposition. Further south US armies were well established on German soil. The US 1st and 9th Armies captured the towns of Julich and Duren and came within sight of the spires of Cologne cathedral, and the whole of General Patton's 3rd Army was closing up to the Rhine between Coblenz and Mannheim. On 7th March the *Eastern Daily Press* headlined its front page:

COLOGNE CAPTURED BY 1ST ARMY

Cologne was captured in twenty-four hours, with little resistance. The defence had been feeble and only 150,000 civilians remained in the city. Reuters' correspondent reported that "street after street is utterly impassable. Cologne is a dead city, eerie in its silence and utter devastation."

On the same day it was reported from the eastern front that the Red Army had reached the mouth of the Oder, and from Burma that the 14th Army was poised to make its final assault on Mandalay. Capture of Mandalay by the 33rd Indian Corps (which included the 2nd British Division of which the Royal Norfolks were a part) was reported on 21st March.

In the west, Allied armies were everywhere closing up to the Rhine. US forces came up to the river opposite Dusseldorf on 3rd March and found all the bridges destroyed, but five days later they captured a virtually intact railway bridge at Remegen, thirty miles south of Cologne. By 9th March the American army was in Bonn, and the *Eastern Daily Press* front page announced:

AMERICANS ACROSS THE RHINE

"Solid bridgehead" held at Remagen

William Stock, the Chelmsford hospital worker, wrote in his diary: "The exciting news has come quicker than I expected. Almost everyone expects the war to be over soon."[4]

By 12th March the Americans had taken 343,000 German prisoners. By the 27th all Germany west of the Rhine was in Allied hands, except for a diminishing triangle between Ludwigshaven and Lauterburg. The time had now come for an assault crossing of the Rhine in the north. For weeks Allied air forces had maintained heavy air raids on the area from Bremen to Koblenz, seeking to isolate this front from the rest of Germany. Two thousand guns were in position to bombard the German defences before the crossing began.

Montgomery's plan was that eighty thousand men would force river crossings at ten different points along a twenty mile front. The 2nd British and the 9th US Armies would seize bridgeheads north and south of Wesel, and the 1st British Commando Brigade, moving between them, would capture the town. After the initial crossings, two airborne divisions—the 6th British and the 17th American—would drop behind the enemy lines. The Canadian army would protect the left flank and cross later.

The 3rd Division took over a stretch of the west bank of the Rhine opposite Emmerich and Rees on 12th March. The 1st Royal Norfolk Battalion, which had been given a few days' rest after the battle for Kervenheim, moved down to the west bank near Till, opposite Emmerich and Dornich, and the 1st Battalion Suffolks took over a nearby area at Kalkar. They spent the remaining fortnight helping with the preparations: the great build-up of tanks, bridging material and stores; the establishment of ammunition, petrol and food dumps; and the movement of craft up to the river. All this activity was kept under cover of a smoke-screen maintained daily until the actual crossing. The men from the eastern counties thus had a spectator's grandstand view of the preparations for, and then the actual crossing of, the Rhine.

> Conditions contrasted completely, and very happily, with their winter vigil by the Maas. The riverside villages were undamaged. Fields that had been flooded were drying in the stronger sun. The nights were shorter, and each morning found new buds on the fruit trees in gardens where snowdrops grew. In this rural life was a fantastic illusion of peace . . .[5]

Their own tasks involved clearing the springboard area between the river and the Kleve – Kalkar – Xanten road of all civilians, cattle and livestock—and seeing they didn't return—and denying the enemy all access to the west bank. At night they posted companies along the river bank to watch for German patrols trying to cross. A few made the attempt, but were either killed on their way over or captured after crossing. Most of the time it was quiet, with very little shelling or other interference from the enemy. Allied bombers and fighters flew continuously overhead, hammering the German defences.

The signal for the final phase of the war was given by Montgomery on 23rd March: "21 Army Group will now cross the Rhine." It was a fine warm day like early summer, a perfect evening for the operation. In two separate raids the RAF blasted Wesel, and late in the afternoon the guns opened up, building in a crescendo over a period of four hours. An officer who was there recalled:

> The din was deafening. It was like one prolonged peal of thunder . . . It was impossible to hear whether any shells were coming the wrong way, but in fact there was little retaliation. The sappers blasted great holes in the bank to allow the Buffaloes to go through, and the Highland Division crossed at 9 p.m.[6]

The Buffaloes were amphibious tracked vehicles, each carrying a platoon of infantry. They ran down into the river and floated across it. Tanks swam over to give armoured support, and reinforcements were ferried over on huge rafts while the Royal Engineers erected the first bridges. By dawn bridgeheads were firmly held. The Commandos were in Wesel, which was captured easily, with only thirty-six casualties.

Part of the Airborne Division dropped that morning was the 9th Parachute Battalion which had been formed early in 1943 from the 10th battalion of the Essex Regiment. They emplaned at dawn at Gosfield in thirty-five Dakotas, and they were dropped behind Wesel at 10 am. After fulfilling their role there they joined the Allied advance on foot.

Within forty-eight hours the first British and Canadian assaults, at Wesel and Rees, were followed by many more crossings to the north and south. After two or three days of hard fighting the enemy resistance was broken and thereafter the German armies never recovered. By 28th March all the main Allied forces had

Opposite: Battalions of the Royal Norfolk and Suffolk Regiments were dug in along the River Maas in January 1944. Once the Rhine has been crossed in late March, the advance into the Reich was rapid. Fierce battles were fought for Kervenheim, Lingum and Brinkum.

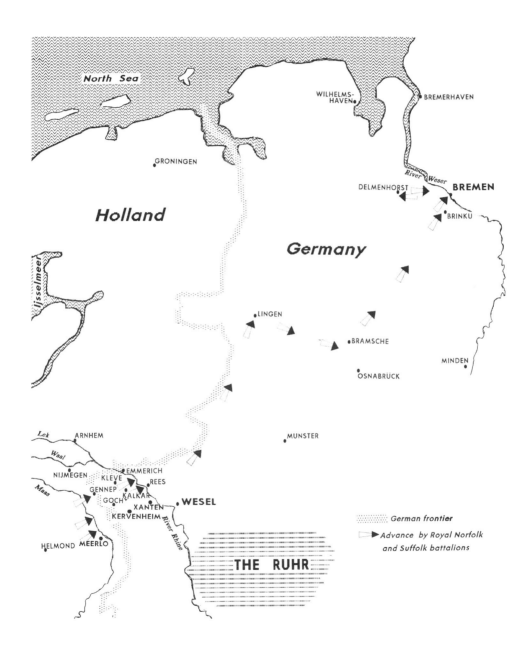

North Sea

WILHELMS-
HAVEN

BREMERHAVEN

GRONINGEN

River Weser

DELMENHORST

BREMEN

Holland

BRINKU

Germany

IJsselmeer

LINGEN

BRAMSCHE

MINDEN

OSNABRÜCK

Lek

ARNHEM

MUNSTER

Waal

NIJMEGEN

EMMERICH

KLEVE

REES

Maas

GENNEP

KALKAR

GOCH

XANTEN

WESEL

KERVENHEIM

River Rhine

German frontier

Advance by Royal Norfolk
and Suffolk battalions

HELMOND

MEERLO

THE RUHR

Cambridge Daily News

crossed the Rhine. After marching to the bridge at Rees, the Suffolk battalion crossed that night, proceeding to the village of Haldern. The Norfolks followed a few hours later, on the 29th.

The advance to the Elbe had already begun with British and American tank spearheads streaming eastwards. The encirclement of the great industrial cities of the Ruhr began: Dusseldorf, Cologne, Essen, Munster, Dortmund, Duisburg, Wuppertal and Hamm, all of them devastated by the earlier Allied bombing raids. Something like 325,000 German troops were trapped; they held out for eighteen days before surrendering. Meanwhile, on the eastern front, the Red Army was making spectacular progress and within a few days was to capture Vienna.

The 3rd Division was ordered to follow up the Guards Armoured Division, consolidating its gains and making itself available should any infantry task arise. The next objective was Bremen. The Royal Norfolks marched northward, keeping close to the Dutch–German frontier, until—at 5 pm on 3rd April—it reached an assembly area for a brigade attack on Lingen, a garrison town and nodal point on the east bank of the Ems Canal. At 7 am next morning a Guards battalion rushed the German defenders and captured the canal bridge intact, and the Norfolks advanced into the town. They took the first half of it in an hour against a half-hearted defence, but then the opposition stiffened and there was a great deal of sniping and resolute street fighting. At nightfall the 2nd Battalion of the Lincolns sent in reinforcements with flame-throwing tanks. After a fairly quiet night there was little fight left in the Germans next day and by noon the town was cleared.

After this ordeal the 1st Battalion Royal Norfolks marched eastward for thirty-five miles without food or sleep to an area south of Bramsche, where they had the 1st Suffolks, with 8 Brigade, on their western flank not far away. The 3rd Division was now established across the main line of retreat of the German 1st Paratroop Army, which had been driven out of Lingen.

It found itself also encountering masses of others in retreat, but streaming westwards. There were thousands of slave-workers conscripted from countries the Nazis had occupied, their few belongings tied to their backs or piled on to handcarts and prams. There were also now thousands of Germans whose homes had been overrun by the Red Army, and who were anxious to end up in territory captured by the British or Americans. Most were women and children, their plight was desperate, and they attracted sympathy. A private in the Suffolk battalion noted:

> Before the collapse of the German army an order was sent out from higher authority to the effect that there was to be no fraternisation with German civilians when we met them in their own country. This, I am afraid, was not seriously observed by the average British soldier. The British Tommy had been noted for his friendliness wherever he was on the continent, and I make no apology that even I felt such an order was alien to the Britisher . . .
>
> I saw little German girls with their two plaits of hair, which was fair, hanging around our cookhouse, grateful to be given even a loaf of bread that had gone stale, and many of the men used to speak and have fun with them, tying their plaits into knots. They were delightful youngsters and we felt sorry for them . . .[7]

Gliders seen on the ground after landing in support of Montgomery's troops who crossed the Rhine at Wesel on 24th March. *Photo courtesy of Ian Hawkins*

By mid-April the 3rd Division had reached the lower Weser, astride which stood the great port of Bremen. The situation there was exceptionally fluid. Allied advance forces had left behind pockets of German troops, and as the division began to close in from the south it met bitter opposition from some of Hitler's crack units—"poor, desperate, frenzied men, bestial, with no decency left in them"[8].

The next planned operation for 8 Brigade (including the Suffolks) and 185 Brigade (including the Royal Norfolks) was the capture of Brinkum, the last small town before the marshes and floods that protected Bremen from the south.

The attack began on Friday, the 13th; 8 Brigade set off along the main road to Brinkum, the Suffolks leading. All went well until they were just a mile-and-a-half short of the town. Their final objective for the day was a cross-roads and as they approached it, in Bren gun carriers and trucks, they ran into cross-fire. Two platoons got over the cross-roads and dug in as it grew dark, and the Germans brought up reinforcements and dug in around the Suffolks. Next day the Suffolks encountered fierce opposition and progress was slow, with confused hand-to-hand fighting, until flame-throwers were brought up and drove the Germans from their trenches.

On the 15th a two-brigade attack was directed at Brinkum; the Warwicks and Norfolks of 185 Brigade approached the town from the right, across open country that was crossed with much difficulty, and the Suffolks of 8 Brigade pushed forward from the cross-roads, aided by tanks and flame-throwers.

It fell to the Warwicks and the Suffolks to share the bitter fighting for the town. As they went forward support artillery hit the streets ahead of them. The Germans fought fanatically and a fierce house-to-house battle continued for three days, until tanks had squirted flame into every house and trench. Only then were the Germans driven out. This victory was gained at a high cost and the loss of British lives at this late stage of the war was regarded as a hard burden to accept.

From Brinkum the city of Bremen could clearly be seen across the flooded fields, and the third week of April was spent in driving the Germans back over this flooded land.

Families back in East Anglia were given some information about their menfolk's activities. The *Eastern Daily Press* carried headlines on 17th April:

BUILDING UP FOR FINAL ELBE BATTLE

Royal Norfolks and Suffolks lead assault on Bremen

The 3rd Division formed up along the line of a flooded area four miles from the city, and the night before the attack Bremen was subjected to a heavy raid by RAF bombers. The assault on the city began on 24th April, when infantry brigades crossed the flooded field in Buffaloes. The Norfolks—who had had a grandstand view of the preliminary RAF bombing—were on the extreme right flank. They went in at 2 pm and found hardly any opposition, and by nightfall they had consolidated a position in the city outskirts. A lone officer, Lieutenant A. R. Gill, went ahead to reconnoitre the route to be taken next morning. After four hours' absence, when a patrol was just about to set off to search for him, he returned leading a column of about one hundred German soldiers who had surrendered to him. He had penetrated three miles into the city.

The next day, 26th April, the 3rd Division broke into Bremen, encountered no opposition, and by 1 pm had captured and secured all its objectives. The city had been completely wrecked. By the evening German civilians began to emerge from shelters and ruined homes to stare impassively at their conquerors.

There was to be no more fighting for the men of this division. Everyone knew the war was as good as over. Both the 1st Royal Norfolk and the 1st Suffolk Battalions moved to the area of Delmenhorst, a few miles to the west, and it was there they heard the news of the cease-fire. The German troops they encountered readily surrendered, while the local population looked on. The Norfolks found themselves in charge of a ridge from which could be seen all the low-lying land up to the river Weser. An army press release described it as "a gunman's dream", adding: "At one period great streams of the enemy could be seen moving west as hard as they could go. Guns fired and the Germans were watched going to ground as shells screamed just over their heads.

Later the Norfolks marched back into Bremen. Civilians appeared by degrees from their hiding places, with set faces. Liberated Poles, French, Czechs and Russian slave-workers made merry. The battalion had difficulty finding shelter until they came upon Beck's brewery, one of the few buildings in that city that was not a mere shell. They immediately installed a company of men for guard duties, and they remained in occupation until most of the contents had been dealt with!

While the 3rd Division was thus engaged in the advance from the Rhine to Bremen, the 2nd Battalion of the Essex Regiment was part of a force which liberated Holland. There there had been a virtual famine throughout the winter, with people existing on one or two slices of bread and a few potatoes every day. They had had no coal, gas or electricity. Half a million Dutch men and boys had been sent to work in German factories. The situation was desperate.

Once the British and American armies were established east of the Rhine, a high priority was given to the recapture of Arnhem and the liberation of north and west Holland. On the night of 12th/13th April the 2nd Glosters crossed the Ijssel river and established an Arnhem bridgehead. The 2nd Essex was one of two battalions which then passed into the heart of the town, supported by the flails, flame-throwers and tanks of the 79th Armoured Division. There was some street fighting and the Germans shelled from high ground outside the town, but the opposition was easily overcome and the clearing up was completed by 14th April. The 2nd Essex then took Velp, a village north-east of Arnhem and its garrison of about one hundred disorganized and dispirited Germans without a single Essex casualty. The battalion returned to Arnhem, embarked in landing craft and moved down the lower Rhine to Wageningem, where they were separated from the enemy lines by two smaller rivers, the Grebbe and the Eem. The war front here was static, and though the Essex battalion did extensive patrolling it was otherwise inactive.

With the capture of Arnhem the Germans in north Holland had been isolated. Negotiations with them led to a truce from 25th April which enabled supplies to be sent into the enemy-held territory. The route for the relief lorries was through the 2nd Essex town of Wageningem. Their Commanding Officer, Lieutenant Colonel E. S. Scott, recalled:

> We had to allow a few German officers to come over under a white flag to this village to arrange details of the truce. Prince Bernhard of the Netherlands came with the Allied officers and a meeting took place in the village hall. After the details of the truce and safe conduct of the lorries had been arranged, the German officers had to be returned to their own lines . . . [9]

In the same village of Wageningen German officers signed an instrument of surrender of all German forces in Holland on 5th May, and the 49th Division—of which the 2nd Essex was part—then moved into the remainder of the country and was given a tumultuous welcome. They occupied the area of Utrecht-Amersfoot. Men of the Essex battalion concentrated in the area of Ziest where, with the 2nd Glosters, they were responsible for the concentration and disarmament of 9,700 men of the German 346th Infantry Division.

Another battalion of the Essex Regiment—the 5th—had joined 21st Army in north-west Europe early in March, having been moved from the Middle East. It had recently come under the command of Lieutenant Colonel W. A. Heal, Suffolk Regiment, and new drafts had brought into its ranks men from forty-one other regiments. Despite this dilution the Essex ethos had survived. Many of the men had been pre-war Territorials together. Their new CO noted that off-duty they tended to gather by district, the men from Saffron Walden in one corner, those of Chelmsford in another, and so on[10].

By the time the 5th Essex moved forward to join the forces on the Elbe on 22nd April most of the fighting was over. The 15th (Scottish) Division established a small bridgehead over the Elbe at Luneberg at the end of April and the 9th Parachute Battalion then enlarged it. The Essex battalion crossed to this bridgehead on a pontoon bridge on 1st May. The plan was to break out as soon as possible and to make for Lubeck, to get across the south of the Schleswig-Holstein peninsula and through to the Baltic coast before the cease-fire. Accordingly, the 9th Parachute Battalion embussed before dawn on 2nd May and travelled sixty miles to Wismar, which was well to the east of Lubeck. It arrived there a few hours before the leading Russian tanks rolled in from Rostock.

The 5th Essex followed behind, and had no contact with Germans except for those trying to surrender. When they arrived at Molln, about eighteen miles due south of Lubeck, a German general staff officer arrived at battalion headquarters and offered to surrender the entire 245th Infantry Division, which was dug in on the line of the Essex advance. The surrender was happily accepted and within three hours about 1,500 prisoners passed through the Essex prisoner-of-war cage. Following this diversion the battalion moved on again. After only a few miles, at Ratzeburg, it found chaos, with Germans wanting to surrender faster than the battalion could cope with them.

Next day two other battalions covered the remaining fifteen miles to Lubeck, but the 5th Essex stopped short of the city, at Grosse Gronau, where they were given the task of sweeping the whole area and bringing in any Germans who had not given themselves up. On the first day they collected six thousand prisoners-of-war in the battalion cage and passed four generals through to division. In due time the Essex men arrived in Wismar, where they relieved the 9th Parachute Battalion which then returned to the UK.

The plan to close off Schleswig-Holstein and access to Denmark from the Russians had succeeded. On 8th May a Suffolk man, Major General R. H. Dewing—whose home was at Lidgate and who was one of three soldier sons of the former (and late) rector of Stowlangtoft—landed by air in Copenhagen as Montgomery's representative, to arrange final details of the German capitulation.

Meanwhile US forces had reached the Elbe just south of Wittenberge, where they were less than eighty-five miles from Berlin, and American and Soviet troops linked up on 25th April. General Eisenhower reached an agreement with the Soviet High Command that the US forces would not move on the capital but would push south and east, and so it was left to Russian troops to complete the encirclement of Berlin. On the 30th the Red Flag was raised over the Reichstag building.

At 3.30 pm that day Hitler shot himself in his bunker, after naming Grand Admiral Donitz as the new Fuhrer. Mussolini had been shot by Italian partisans three days earlier, and his death had been quickly followed by the unconditional surrender of all German troops in Italy.

The Allied armies in Europe now waited for the German High Command to recognize the inevitable. Marshal Zhukov accepted the surrender of Berlin on 2nd May and that same day the Mayor of Hamburg began negotiations for the unconditional surrender of his city.

The favourable war news from all fronts reached East Anglians in big front-page headlines. The *Eastern Daily Press* on 3rd May

GERMAN SURRENDER IN ITALY

Berlin garrison gives in—over 70,000 prisoners taken yesterday

And then, the following day:

RANGOON FALLS

On 4th May German officers came to the Tactical Headquarters of Montgomery's 21st Army Group on Luneburg Heath and signed a surrender document for all German forces in north-west Germany, Denmark and Holland, effective at 8 am the following day. Various surrenders took place elsewhere. On 6th May General Jodl flew from Admiral Donitz's headquarters at Flensburg to Eisenhower's headquarters at Rheims in order to face the Supreme Allied Commander and representatives of the United Kingdom, Russia and France. Asked to sign the capitulation of all German forces still fighting or facing the western Allies, he wriggled a little and referred back to Donitz, but eventually at 2.41 am on 7th May he signed. The surrender came into effect at one minute after midnight on 8th/9th May.

The news that everyone in Britain had eagerly awaited was conveyed in big black type on Tuesday 8th May. The *Eastern Daily Press* streamer across its front page read:

WAR IN EUROPE ENDS—VE DAY TODAY

Flags of Victory decorating Cambridge Guildhall on VE Day.   *Cambridge Daily News*

CHAPTER FOUR

The Setting Sun

IN THE same week that Hitler committed suicide and Germany surrendered, the Japanese army abandoned Rangoon, the capital of Burma, and on 3rd May the 26th Indian Division moved into the city. This success came more easily than the Allied commanders had expected. The plan had been to assault the city from the sea, and for several weeks the 2nd Battalion of the Royal Norfolk Regiment had been training in India as part of the 2nd Division for this important amphibious operation, which was to mark the successful end of the Allied campaign to recapture Burma. The division had been withdrawn by air on 11th April to a tented camp thirty-five miles from Calcutta, and had trained intensively over assault courses and in landing craft. Now the operation was cancelled. The Norfolk men settled in India; their war was over.

During 1944 the men of the battalion had become tough and experienced warriors in the hills and jungle. As the year ended they were part of a force that drove the Japanese back over the Chindwin river at Kalewa and into the Schwebo Plain. Then, until they were sent to India, they had been in the thick of the struggle to destroy an enemy in full retreat across central Burma. Early in 1945 the Royal Norfolks established a record unequalled in the British army during the war when one of its officers, Lieutenant George Arthur Knowland, was awarded the regiment's fifth Victoria Cross.

Knowland died defending a forward position on a hill near Kangaw, where his platoon of twenty-four men was repeatedly attacked by a force of three hundred Japanese. He darted from trench to trench grabbing whatever weapon was to hand, successively firing rifle, Bren gun, mortar and tommy gun, and often revealing himself within ten yards of the enemy in order to improve his line of fire. Fourteen of his twenty-four men were casualties at an early stage and six of his positions were overrun, but the remainder held on through twelve hours of fierce fighting until reinforcements arrived. Before Knowland died he killed or wounded a large number of the enemy. His action was considered to have prevented a serious Japanese incursion and to have made possible a successful counter-attack from the ground he had held.

Once the Norfolks moved into the Schwebo Plain and were on their way to Mandalay, they had to adapt to a different kind of warfare. This was open country with low hills and no shelter from the blazing sun. Infantry and armour moved at speed, rations and ammunition being dropped to forward units from the air and British and US fighter planes encountered very little opposition. The attempt to

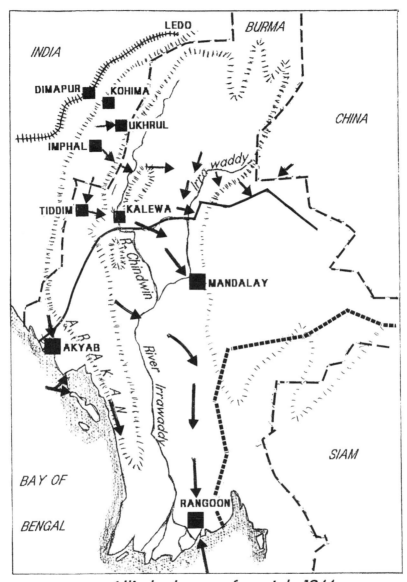

→ → *Allied advances from July 1944*

―――― *Allied Line at December 31, 1944*

·········· *Allied Line at June 18, 1945*

╫╫╫╫╫╫╫ *Rail link to India*

destroy the Japanese in the plain was unsuccessful, however, and they withdrew in good order across the Irrawaddy river in the area of Mandalay.

Part of the enemy force held on for a time in a bend of the Irrawaddy westward of Sagaing, and the Norfolks formed part of a brigade that was given the task of eliminating this pocket of resistance. It was parched and inhospitable country of rocky, sandy, undulating scrub, but the sector was important to the Japanese because it covered the river opposite Mandalay, and they kept it under heavy shellfire. The Norfolks pressed forward, supported by tanks. After hard fighting in intense heat they crossed the river in DUKWS and helped to expand a bridgehead established by another brigade two days earlier.

Mandalay was captured by the 19th (Indian) Division during 9th/10th March while the 2nd Division—of which the Royal Norfolks were part—captured a series of villages and cleared the areas to the south, often moving through tall elephant grass that limited visibility to ten yards. The battalion then had a week's rest. They swam in the river and visited Mandalay—though that offered no pleasures, for the town had been almost totally destroyed by fire. An army film unit recorded the activities of two score of the men during this period, and the Army Welfare authorities arranged for the film to be shown to the men's families in the Haymarket Cinema in Norwich in July.

The 14th Army next moved southward down the Sittang valley to Meiktila, and thence to Rangoon. The 2nd Division, including the Norfolks, was sent ahead to prepare the way for an advance, but it had scarcely got moving before it was reassigned to the proposed amphibious operation and withdrawn and flown to India.

The 2nd Battalion of the Suffolk Regiment also moved forward from the Chindwin river into the Schwebo Plain during the early weeks of 1945. It came within a few miles of the Irrawaddy, but its ordeal during 1944—when it had played a leading role in expelling Japanese invaders from India and then driving them back to the Chindwin—had taken a heavy toll. The battalion was weak in numbers and in March it was flown out of the operational area and back to India.

With the capture of Rangoon the situation in South East Asia was transformed. The year had begun with the reopening after three years of the Burma Road—the land route to China. From January American Fortresses had regularly bombed Singapore Island, and now British bombers extended their operations. In June they destroyed two railway bridges over the river Kwai in Siam, which Allied prisoners-of-war had been forced to build in 1942–3; in July they bombed Japanese troops trying to escape from south Burma through Moulmein, and killed ten thousand of them.

After the capture of Rangoon the 14th Army continued to advance southwards and by the time the European war was ending, in early May, it had liberated four hundred British, American and Indian prisoners-of-war from Japanese camps. During the twelve months it had taken to reconquer Burma, more than one hundred thousand Japanese had been killed in action and thousands more had died of disease and privation.

Burma was but a small part of the three million square miles of territory the Japanese had occupied after entering the war by their attack on the US navy at Pearl Harbour in December 1941. Final Allied victory over Japan could only be achieved by the American forces deployed across the vast Pacific area, and would involve occupation of the Japanese home islands. When the war in Europe ended that seemed a long way off.

By the beginning of 1945 the Americans had recaptured the two Philippine islands of Leyte and Mindoro; in January they landed on the central island of Luzon; and on 23rd February they occupied Manila, the capital. It was in ruins, and the Japanese had murdered nearly one hundred thousand Filipino civilians there[1]. At about the same time the capture of the island of Iwo Jima gave them a base from which they could bomb the Japanese home islands 750 miles away. On 9th March they directed against Tokyo "the most destructive single bombing raid yet known" and created a bigger firestorm than the RAF had caused at Dresden. Over the following months many other big cities were bombed and more than 250,000 civilians killed.

American gains were achieved only at tremendous cost. The Japanese fought fanatically, refusing to surrender, and turned every street and every building into a bloody battleground. Their apparent indifference to their own losses found ultimate expression in the behaviour of kamikaze pilots who crashed explosive-packed planes on to selected targets.

War against Japan

You must see this
EXHIBITION

CAVENDISH LABORATORY
FREE SCHOOL LANE
Open Weekdays only until
SATURDAY, JULY 14th
from 10 a.m.—5.30 p.m.
ADMISSION FREE

"War Against Japan"—A reminder that the war was not over.   *Cambridge Daily News*

Corregidor Island was captured by the Americans amid scenes of carnage. Mindanao was invaded on 10th March, but Japanese resistance there did not end until 25th July. Similarly they fought on Okinawa from 1st April until 21st June, making it the greatest land battle of the Pacific war. The US lost 12,500 of the fifty thousand troops it put ashore, but ninety thousand of a Japanese garrison of one hundred thousand were wiped out and altogether half a million people were believed to have died—half of them Japanese and the other half Okinawans. Here one of the most horrific events of the war occurred, when eighty-five Japanese student nurses who had been caught in the fighting retreated, terrified, into a cave.

> Marines reaching the mouth of the cave heard Japanese voices within. They did not recognise the tones as feminine, and neither did their interpreter, who demanded that those inside emerge at once. When they didn't, flame-throwers, moving in, killed them all. To this day, Japanese come to mourn at what is now known as the "Cave of the Virgins".[2]

Early in July, when air and sea bombardment of the Japanese home islands had become an almost daily event, the Americans moved into a "pre-invasion stage". They fixed 1st November as the date for an invasion of Japan's southernmost island of Kyushu, and had in mind 1st March 1946 for an invasion of the principal island of Honshu[3].

In the United States, however, scientists had opened up a new possibility. They had developed and tested an atom bomb, and with this new weapon at his disposal President Truman, with Churchill's concurrence (the British Pacific Fleet was now involved in the assault on Japan), despatched a message to Tokyo demanding unconditional surrender, the alternative being "complete and utter destruction".

There was no response and at 8.15 am local time on 6th August an atom bomb was dropped on Hiroshima. Eighty thousand people were killed and thirty-five thousand injured, and of the ninety thousand buildings in the city, 62,000 were destroyed. Another atom bomb was dropped on Nagasaki on 9th August at 11.02 am local time, and about forty thousand were reported killed. On the same day as the Nagasaki bomb the Soviet Union declared war on Japan and invaded Japanese Manchuria.

The use of the atom bombs caused considerable controversy, and even the scientists and military men seemed awed by their destructive power. Thirty years after the war ended the number of identified victims in Hiroshima was estimated at 138,890, with people still dying of radiation. The full death toll in Nagasaki was estimated at 48,857. Churchill mused: "The revelation of the secrets of Nature, long mercifully withheld from Man, should arouse the most solemn reflection in the mind and conscience of every human being capable of comprehension."[4] Reflection in the mind of the Bishop of Chelmsford, Dr Henry Wilson, led him to the view, expressed in his *Diocesan Chronicle*, that:

> It is quite impossible with any consistency to defend this kind of warfare. When the flying bombs and rockets were falling on us, we charged the Germans with the indiscriminate

slaughter of non-combatants. That is precisely what the Allied Nations have done to a degree a hundred times greater than did the Nazis.

The justification for using the atom bombs was expressed by the British Supreme Commander in South East Asia, Admiral Lord Louis Mountbatten, in these words:

> I am responsible for trying to kill as many Japanese as I can with the minimum of loss on our side. War is crazy. It is a crazy thing that we are fighting at all. But it would be even more crazy if we were to have more casualties on our side to save the Japanese.[5]

Churchill told the Commons that without the atom bombs the Pacific war might have cost one million American and 250,000 British lives.

Before the Americans had time to drop their first atom bomb, the US cruiser *Indianapolis*, which had carried it from the United States to the Pacific, was torpedoed. Just before midnight on 29th July, only three days after it delivered its lethal cargo, the Japanese sent it to the bottom of the Pacific. More than 350 of its crew were killed in the explosion and 484 died in the water, drowned or eaten by sharks. Only 318 survived this, "the greatest loss at sea in the history of the US Navy"[6].

After the atom bombs the Americans showered three million leaflets on to Japan. "Petition your Emperor to end the war", they read. "Take steps now, or we shall resolutely employ this bomb promptly and forcefully."[7] Within hours the *Eastern Daily Press* was reporting on its front page:

JAPANESE OFFER TO SURRENDER

The Allied leaders received the Japanese acceptance of unconditional surrender with great caution, and four days passed before terms were agreed. In Britain the new Prime Minister, Clement Attlee, then broadcast the news, and 15th and 16th August were designated VJ-Days. Some fighting continued after that, and the Japanese commander in Burma did not confirm the cease-fire until 23rd August.

The major Japanese surrender ceremony took place on board the US battleship *Missouri* in Tokyo Bay on 2nd September. Ten days later, in Singapore, Lord Louis Mountbatten took the formal surrender of all Japanese forces within the South East Asia Command.

The first man of the British occupation forces to set foot on Japanese soil was from Norwich. He was Lieutenant Colin Canham, DSO, who was commanding a party of sailors from the cruiser *Newfoundland*, which was anchored in Tokyo Bay.

The end of the war in the Far East had special significance for the people of East Anglia. Seven battalions of soldiers from the eastern counties had been captured by the Japanese at the fall of Singapore in February 1942 and had since been held in prisoner-of-war camps: the 4th and 5th Battalions of the Suffolk Regiment; the 1st and 2nd Battalions of the Cambridgeshire Regiment; and the 4th, 5th and 6th Battalions of the Royal Norfolk Regiment. A large number of them had been drafted into Siam to help construct a railway link with Burma, but

General Numuta Takazo leads the Japanese delegation to the signing of the surrender of the Japanese southern army, at Rangoon, 28th August.   *Imperial War Museum*

when this was completed in 1943 only a small number were retained for maintenance. The remainder had been dispersed to Japan and occupied territories all over the Pacific, split into small detachments with officers segregated from men.

It was only now, with the war over, that the world heard of the hardships they had endured. Captain R. M. Oliver of the 5th Suffolks gave an account of a voyage from Singapore to Saigon in a 3,500–ton Japanese transport:

> We finally left [Singapore] on February 2nd; our party included the Dutch, a small Australian party, and ourselves—about 2,500 prisoners-of-war. We marched to the docks and found we were all to travel together on one ship; but to make matters worse, there were 750 Javanese coolies on board already. The Japanese had attempted to rig up the "between decks" with bunks to hold 300, but, by forcing people below and knocking them down with rifle butts, they managed to crowd in 600 . . . To make matters worse, the [vessel] had a very large deck cargo of lorries, steam-rollers, hen coops, and all the rubbish and filth that only can accumulate in Japanese ships.[8]

The heat was stifling, the men were bathed in sweat all day, and the only washing "facility" was a salt water hose, for the use of which men queued for hours. They were given half a pint of tea twice a day and two rice meals. Some were ill with heat stroke and dysentery; ten Javanese coolies died. This ship, one of three, escorted by three Japanese warships reached Saigon on 7th February. Two others in the convoy were torpedoed[9].

A number of Japanese prison ships were similarly torpedoed, usually by the American navy; an officer and ninety men of the 2nd Battalion of the Suffolks died in one such incident. There were Allied casualties, too, when planes began to bomb the Burma–Siam railway which the prisoners-of-war had built.

Conditions in almost all the Japanese camps were appalling. Food was scarce; the Allied blockade of sea routes prevented many ships from reaching Singapore. At the Changi Camp in Singapore over eighty per cent of prisoners suffered from vitamin deficiency illnesses, and malnutrition or beri-beri had reduced some to a condition in which they were unable to walk. Many were eating roots and frogs[10].

Most of the prisoners-of-war knew something of the progress of the war in 1945. In spite of frequent searches by the Japanese, home-made wireless sets were in operation. The news spread that Germany had been defeated, and hopes soared. Then early in August they were able to make deductions from the changing attitude of the Japanese prison guards in some of the camps—there was less brutality. Some of the guards disappeared and were replaced by new faces. At many camps the Japanese burned documents on the parade ground. By the middle of the month every camp was buzzing with rumours. When surrender came prisoners in some camps were paraded and given the news by their own officers. At Changi two British Liberators flew low over the camp on 26th August dropping leaflets. Altogether thirty-three million leaflets were dropped on ninety camps in northern Malaya, Burma and Siam and on 150 other localities explaining that the war was over and that help was on its way.

A few days later medical officers and supplies were parachuted into the camps. Swiss officials of the Red Cross were the first to arrive at Changi, with seventy-four lorries carrying food and clothing. British paratroops landed three days later with medical supplies[11]. Gradually all prisoners were brought down to centres where they could be re-equipped with clothes and properly housed. They were given their letters from home and vitamin pills with every meal. The paratroops left and officials of an organization known as RAPWI (Repatriation of Allied Prisoner-of-War Internees) took over[12].

Families of these prisoners-of-war received little, if any, news during the war of their whereabouts and welfare. The *Eastern Daily Press*, reporting on 3rd January that Mrs Mary Boast of Norwich had received a letter from her husband, with his photograph, stated that this was believed to be the first photograph ever to reach Britain of a prisoner-of-war in Japanese hands. For over a year Mrs Boast had heard nothing at all of her thirty-three-year-old husband, who was in the Suffolk Regiment; then she received eight postcards and a letter in a single week and learned that he was held in a camp at Hakodate in Japan. In the first few days of January several families received postcards postmarked over seven months earlier.

The regimental families' associations did their best for the families that were in suspense. For example there was a party early in the new year for one hundred children, some with their mothers or grandmothers, of men of the Cambridgeshire Regiment who were prisoners. British Legion clubs organized monthly meetings for relatives, and the Red Cross did its best to pass on whatever information came to hand. A special journal, *Far East*, was circulated to the relatives of Cambridgeshire Regiment prisoners-of-war. In March families were invited to send ten-word telegrams to prisoners; about two thousand were being despatched each week but no one was sure how many were received by the men at the other end. The Ministry of Information organized an exhibition called "War Against Japan" which toured the eastern counties during the summer.

After the Japanese surrender families waited happily but impatiently. On 21st August the *Eastern Daily Press* front page had a report headlined "Arrangements for moving Far East Prisoners-of-war", but there were no specific details so the story had a teasing and frustrating effect. The *Cambridge Daily News* stated on 1st September:

> It is reasonable to expect that the great majority of the 1,648 men of the 2nd battalion of the Cambridgeshire Regiment who fell into Japanese hands will have survived their captivity . . . It is expected that telegrams bringing joy and hope to many at home will soon be to hand".

Again, there was little specific detail to allay the anxieties of families. There was one clear announcement—from the government—that was helpful: ex-prisoners-of-war from the Far East would be allowed to leave the services as soon as their repatriation leave ended.

A report of the first mass release dominated the front page of the *Cambridge Daily News* on 1st September:

20,000 SINGAPORE P.O.W. ARE FREED
6,500 BRITONS AMONG THEM

It said that a relief party had been dropped from the air and had released the men in five camps. The same day the first direct message arrived from an individual member of the Cambridgeshire Regiment; Mrs Unwin of Histon received a cablegram from her husband, Captain Philip Unwin, announcing that he was safe and well in Bangkok.

Throughout September lists of families who had received news were published daily, and the big front-page stories concerned the liberated prisoners. On the 4th it was reported that seventy-four Super Forts had dropped more than two hundred tons of supplies to prison camps on the Japanese home islands of Honshu and Kyushu.

Ronald Searle, released from Japanese captivity, sent readers of the *Cambridge Daily News* this "cheery cartoon from the Far East".
Cambridge Daily News

On the 8th there were these hopeful headlines:

ALL PoW'S OUT OF JAPAN IN A MONTH

1,500 are leaving every day

PARTIES HUNTING FOR PRISON CAMPS

Most of the messages now seemed reassuring in that men were reported to be fitter than had been expected. Miss Mary C. Gray, a former regional administrator of the Women's Voluntary Service in the eastern region, had become a WVS welfare officer at SEAC Headquarters, and she wrote to the *Cambridge Daily News* reporting that the Cambridgeshire men she had met were "well, considering all they have been through, and most of them look remarkably fit". The paper also received a message at about the same time from its pre-war cartoonist, Sapper Ronald Searle, reporting his "pretty ghastly experience". He was just about to be discharged from hospital and hoped to leave in a hospital ship in a day or two. He wrote: "I have put on about 2 lbs a day since the Red Cross stuff came in the other week . . . I am still drawing and drawing. Hope to have some very useful stuff by the time I get home."

A little later he wrote again, enclosing a cartoon. He related that the MP journalist Tom Driberg, who was visiting Singapore, had introduced him to Mountbatten and his wife:

> They took myself and two other friends down to Government House, where we had dinner with them and their red-tabbed, gold-braided, beribboned chiefs of staff—about 40 altogether . . . I was dressed like this: an old cardigan, one piece of blue silk as a scarf, ancient shorts and a pair of cut-down Japanese boots (my entire wardrobe at that moment, September 14th) . . . A few hours before I was in my cell.

Searle did not reach England until mid-October. In December an exhibition of his sketches was put on at Cambridge Technical College. Some works had been executed on scraps of stolen paper and his brushes had been made with hair from stray cats that had been killed for food.

Some men began their journey home by plane to Rangoon and India, some by ship to America, others to Australia and thence to Southampton and Liverpool. Only a small number were flown home. News of those returning by sea trickled out little by little. On 14th September it was reported that men of a battalion of the Royal Norfolks had reached India and were waiting there to be repatriated; a week later the news was that some Cambridgeshire men had sailed from Colombo on the 20th on the liner *Monowai*, due at Plymouth on 10th October.

The War Office announced that by 20th September twenty-five thousand ex-prisoners and five thousand civilian internees had left the countries in which they had been held and were on the first stage of their journey back to Britain. Another report disclosed that men of the Royal Norfolk and Cambridgeshire Regiments were among 1,500 liberated prisoners from South East Asia who had arrived at

Colombo and left for the UK by sea. Six other vessels had sailed from India. Other details emerged piecemeal as the days passed.

Then came the big news. On Sunday 7th October the *Corfu*, the first of the repatriation ships to arrive, sailed into Southampton. There were over 1,500 men of fifty different regiments on board, but most of them had fought together in the 18th Division: men of the Royal Norfolks, the Suffolks and the Cambridgeshire. There were only twelve officers and 114 men of the 4th, 5th and 6th Battalions of the Royal Norfolks, however, and but ninety-one men of the Cambridgeshire Regiment.

The returning soldiers received a tremendous welcome. Two former commanding officers of the Cambridgeshire, Lieutenant Colonel F. N. Drake Digby and Colonel M. C. Clayton, went to Southampton, borrowed a US army cutter, went out to meet the *Corfu* in Southampton Water and led her in. Every ship in the Solent blew its siren in greeting, the band of the 60th Rifles played on the quay, and the men on board sang "Tipperary". The Under-Secretary of State for War, Lord Nathan, with the Bishop of Winchester and army brass and civic heads went aboard, and a message was read from the King and Queen. When the men came ashore British Legion veterans presented their banners in salute and WVS workers and many men and women in the crowd pressed cigarettes and chocolates on them.

They were then taken through beflagged streets to a transit camp that had been set up on Southampton Common. The special correspondent of the *Eastern Daily Press* reported that most of the men looked "bronzed and hardened and extremely fit" as a result of good food since their liberation and a healthy sea voyage home. At the transit camp they were all medically examined and issued with ration coupons, travel passes and so on. Special telephone lines had been installed for use by those whose relatives had telephones in their homes. Some relatives travelled to the camp, and a few were successful in making contact there.

The men travelled a day or two later by special trains to London and then dispersed to their homes. When the first party reached Norwich Thorpe station there were several thousand people there to welcome them, crowding the station and the station yard, and lining both sides of Prince of Wales Road for some distance towards the city centre. Many waved Union Jacks, some climbed lamp standards and railings. Relatives were invited through to the arrival platform. There was a high pitch of excitement. The train was expected at 9.30 pm and when some coaches backed into the station at about that time the cheering began. But it was mistimed—the London train was running twenty-nine minutes late.

When it did arrive a woman announcer's voice came over the public address system "The train now arriving is the London train. Hip . . . pip . . . pip . . .". Her voice was drowned by the thousands cheering. On Platform 2 there were emotional reunions and embraces, and constant flashes as the press photographers went into action. The following day batches of ex-prisoners arrived at Thorpe by

BACK TO FAMILIAR GROUNDS

A group of repatriated prisoners of war from the Far East at Thorpe station before being led out of the station by the band of the Royal Norfolks.   *Eastern Daily Press*

almost every train, and the band of the Royal Norfolks was there to lead some of them out of the station.

The arrival of the first party at Cambridge station that same evening was an anti-climax, for only nine officers and men—most of them of the 2nd Battalion of the Cambridgeshire Regiment—turned up. No one knew who would arrive or when. Relatives, members of the Red Cross and St John's Ambulance Brigade, Army Welfare Service representatives and volunteer drivers hung around from lunch-time until 7 pm. Only ten more men arrived the following day and after that there was a mere trickle. Still no one was sure what to expect.

The second repatriation vessel, the *Monowai*, arrived at Liverpool a day later, the first of sixteen ships sailing to that port.

At every arrival at the ports and home towns men and their families were met by the Red Cross and St John's Ambulance Brigade and by representatives of the Territorial Army associations, who had organized private cars to take them to their homes.

Three hundred men of the 2nd Royal Norfolks, the battalion that had fought in Burma until the fall of Rangoon and had then been withdrawn to India, returned to Britain before the year was out. At Thorpe station in Norwich in November they were greeted by the Lord Mayor, Mr S. A. Bailey and several hundred relatives and friends, and then sent on leave until 1st January.

Throughout their captivity, the prisoners managed to keep accurate records of all deaths and burials.

> Lists of casualties were buried in tins, hidden inside Bibles, and sewn up in shirts, and miraculously all these records survived, though many of the authors did not. In this way, the fate of almost every man of the regiment was known as soon as these documents came back to England at the end of the war.[13]

How well the administrative tasks were performed when the survivors reached Britain is illustrated by the example of the men of the Cambridgeshire Regiment. Regimental offices were set up at Cambridge, Ely and Wisbech, and survivors of the headquarters staffs of the two battalions volunteered to spend their leave compiling records and answering enquiries. As they reached home each returning group of ex-prisoners sent in their casualty lists. Within a few weeks complete returns were supplied to the Infantry Record Office, and plans of the various cemeteries in Malaya and Siam were submitted to the War Office. Many hundreds of enquiries were also dealt with[14].

It now became painfully clear how many families had no one to welcome home. Of nearly one thousand of the 5th Battalion of the Suffolk Regiment who went to the Far East, more than a third did not come back. The *Cambridge Daily News* reported on 8th December that there were only 170 to 200 Cambridge ex-prisoners-of-war.

The year ended with reunions of the survivors. In Cambridge by way of a "civic welcome" they were invited—with their wives, mothers or lady friends—to a dance and cabaret in the Guildhall. In Bury St Edmunds over 250 men of the 5th Battalion of the Suffolk Regiment assembled at the Corn Exchange. These were not, and could not be, joyous occasions. At the Bury St Edmunds gathering chilling statistics were read out: of a total of 979 men who went to the Far East, 632 had returned. Thirty-seven had been killed, were missing or had died of wounds sustained in action; 289 had died as prisoners-of-war in Japanese hands; fourteen had been posted missing at sea; and seven were listed as "other losses".

Hardships undergone in the prisoner-of-war camps left a mark on most of the survivors, and many had great difficulty in adjusting to civilian life. Others found they had permanent disabilities that prevented their working again. All returned prisoners-of-war were offered month-long retraining courses at a civil resettlement unit, either before or after their demobilization. Most of the East Anglians who took advantage of the offer went to Acton Place, a manor house near Sudbury. It had been a US army hospital during the war and the manor house was surrounded by temporary buildings which offered comfortable accommodation. It was one of eighteen such centres in Britain.

CHAPTER FIVE

Celebrating Peace

FOR AN event so desperately yearned for, so constantly dreamt of, and so long awaited the celebration of victory was a remarkably ragged affair. Anyone who had anticipated great set-piece parades on one special day was disappointed. It could not be like that, if only because the surrender processes were long drawn out and confused. The German surrender of Berlin to the Russians took place on 2nd May, the formal surrender to the Combined Allied Powers took place at Eisenhower's headquarters in the early hours of 7th May; but Churchill's broadcast to the nation proclaiming victory did not come until 3 pm on 8th May. Then, although the German armies in Europe had surrendered, the Japanese appeared still to have a great deal of fight left in them and a significant body of men from East Anglia were still their prisoners-of-war. When fighting ceased in the Far East there was, as we have seen, more confusion and uncertainty; the Japanese offered unconditional surrender on 10th August, but the formal peace declarations were not made until noon on the 15th.

Families in Britain saw the first real evidence that the war was in its final phase when some of the men fighting in Europe were granted home leave early in January. Hundreds of people gathered at Victoria station to give a joyously noisy welcome to the troop trains.

Many towns and villages then established "Welcome Home" committees, to plan for the return of those in the services when the war ended. The purpose of these committees was not often well defined, and confusion and controversy arose. A spokesman for the village of Strumpshaw suggested that—as well as organizing dances, whist drives and concerts—they would give each returning member of the forces a share of the fund as a gift. The rector of Garboldisham, the Reverend N. R. M. Hawthorn, who had been serving abroad for three years, wrote to the *Eastern Daily Press* declaring:

> The soldier on his return chiefly wants to find his wife faithful, his children well cared for, and his home intact from bombing . . . Beyond this, he hopes for speedy demobilisation and a secure job. He will not expect to be treated as a hero. Above all, he will actively resent anything savouring of charity.

This point was reinforced at the Suffolk county conference of the British Legion at Ipswich in March by Major E. L. D. Lake. Speaking of "Homecoming Funds", he said, "It would be utterly repugnant to those now serving to attempt to value their services by giving them a small dole out of a war charity."

58

The first troops from Europe come on leave during January. This advertisement—"Help to cheer the boys on their way"—sought recruits to the N.A.A.FI.

Eastern Daily Press

HELP to cheer the boys on their way

On Miss Naffy's ready shoulders falls yet another task. When the boys come home on leave, no effort is spared to ease the burden of the journey. As the men speed homeward, Naafi girls on the leave trains serve tea and snacks in special buffet cars.

Others were concerned that fund-raising by these local committees would be at the expense of British Legion and official county war charities. The *Eastern Daily Press*, in a leading article, commented: "In the end, what will certainly happen in the great majority of cases will be that the monies collected will be dissipated on mere bean-feasting of no permanent benefit to anyone."

The Lord Lieutenant of Suffolk, the Earl of Stradbroke, launched a County Remembrance Fund which, he said, would distribute help in every case of need through such bodies as the British Legion; the Soldiers', Sailors' and Airmen's Families Association; and the regimental funds. He invited the Local Welcome Home committees to pass over the money they had collected. These differences had not been resolved by the time the war ended.

Plans for VE-Day took definite shape, however, and were announced well in advance. Norwich made it known that emphasis would be on thanksgiving rather than celebration. The general mood was clearly shown when Newmarket Urban District Council members agreed that celebrations would be inappropriate while local men were Japanese prisoners-of-war, and decided that there would only be thanksgiving services in churches.

Cambridge Town Council voted one hundred pounds to the Mayor and three hundred pounds to the entertainments committee to cover the costs of a programme of events and, although it showed reluctance to celebrate while 2,200 men from Cambridgeshire remained prisoners of the Japanese, it was severely criticized in some quarters. A correspondent writing to the *Cambridge Daily News* asked: "Have they no sense of decency? This is a town with all its Territorials in enemy hands in the Far East . . .".

Most individuals, however, had private thoughts about the way they would mark the end of the war, and the Mass Observation organization questioned some of its contacts in East Anglia. One replied: "I shall hang out the flags and offer a few drinks to my friends . . . I shall avoid any Mafeking street crowds—I expect there will be too much drinking . . . I hope there will be religious services"[1]. Another responded: "I will confess to have 'mised' [saved] up a bottle of vintage port and a bottle of 30-year-old champagne as a very inadequate way of celebrating. They have been kept since the beginning of the war."[2]

On the morning of 7th May—the day of Germany's official surrender—East Anglia was full of rumours, but no official word came through. Prime Minister Winston Churchill wanted to make the formal announcement that evening and had prepared his words, but Stalin and Truman insisted on delay, and Churchill waited until the following day. Thus it was that newspaper and radio reports made it clear that the war had ended long before there was any official pronouncement, with the result that celebrations began in a strangely tentative way. A report in the *South West Suffolk Echo* relating to the small East Anglian town of Haverhill gives this picture.

> The day was one of tense expectation, when everyone lived from hour to hour for the next bulletin. Radio sets worked overtime; constructive plans were impossible and there was a certain amount of diffidence as to who would make the first sign that the great moment had arrived, until temerarious tradesmen began to make a display of flags and national colours in their windows. Still the Prime Minister had not made the official announcement, and the town was in a state of uncertainty as to whether the evening would be spent in thanksgiving or otherwise . . .

Similarly at Colchester radio news of the German surrender was initially received quietly. "No-one, after all, seemed in the mood for the long-expected and intended revelling", noted one observer. "In the calm of a beautiful Spring evening the crowds strolled in the streets and the Castle Park accustoming themselves to the fact that at last the guns were still."

It was much the same in Norwich. The *Eastern Daily Press* report stated that: "During the morning and early afternoon it seemed that most people were content to relax, quietly and soberly, after the strain and stress of the last 5½ years." But soon the City Hall was covered with flags and streamers; every other person was wearing a red, white and blue rosette or head-band; the church bells began to ring; and then, in the neighbourhood of The Walk and the City Hall, the crowds began to let themselves go. That evening the city was a blaze of light, the City Hall, the Guildhall, the castle and other civic buildings flood-lit. Several searchlights were focused on the cathedral, and a moving searchlight starting from Duke Street picked out in turn all the prominent buildings of the city. The V (for victory) sign was flashed into the sky intermittently until the small hours of the morning.

So it was everywhere: the tremendous emotional release could not be contained and there was a spontaneous outbreak of excitement. Gradually flags, bunting and banners bearing pictures of the King, the Queen and Mr Churchill were decked over houses and cottages all over East Anglia. When darkness fell, RAF and USAAF stations joined in, discharging Verey flares, rockets and fireworks, and aircraft dropped chandeliers of lights. "The sky for miles around resembled the aurora borealis ... an unforgettable fairyland of colour", one newspaper reported.

In Bury St Edmunds the Abbey Gardens were illuminated; there was dancing on Angel Hill; and the streets were thronged with cheering, singing crowds.

In Cambridge a good-humoured crowd of several thousand gathered on Market Square as dusk approached—singing, dancing, cheering and generally giving vent to high spirits. Bonfires were lit in the street. One agile enthusiast climbed to the top of the fountain to hoist the Union Jack, and it was soon joined by the Red Flag and the Stars and Stripes. Spirits did not flag until midnight.

The following day—officially declared VE-Day—a more formal programme was followed. In Cambridge there was a service of thanksgiving in Great St Mary's and then the town was *en fête* with thousands thronging the beflagged and decorated streets and visiting Market Square to dance and cheer. A musical programme began at noon and was kept up all day. Children waved Union Jacks and many people dressed themselves in red, white and blue.

In many towns Winston Churchill's broadcast address was relayed over loud-speakers to large crowds in market squares and other suitable open spaces. This

Halstead Urban District Council.

VE DAY

PUBLIC NOTICE IS GIVEN OF THE FOLLOWING PROPOSED ARRANGEMENTS FOR HALSTEAD:—

(1) The news will be proclaimed from the Market Hill.
(2) A United Service of Thanksgiving will be held in the Public Gardens.
(3) The Braintree Town Band will play in the Public Gardens, which will be illuminated at dusk.
(4) There will be Services of Thanksgiving at 7 p.m. in each Church in the Town.
(5) The broadcast by His Majesty The King will be relayed in the Public Gardens at 9 p.m.
(6) The Church Bells will be rung.

The Public are asked to display flags and decorations and to leave a light burning in a window visible from the highway for thirty minutes after sunset.

The British Restaurant will be closed.

The times of the above events will be announced by radio van.

Advert for Halstead U.D.C. V.E. Day programme. *Dave Osborne* was followed in most places by the appearance of the Mayor in full regalia to add local sentiments to those expressed by the Prime Minister on behalf of the nation.

As the clock on Great St Mary's in Cambridge struck 4 pm the Town Crier, in scarlet robes, appeared on the balcony of the beflagged Guildhall, followed by the Mayor, Councillor George Wilding; the Rural Dean; the Lord Lieutenant; the Vice-Chancellor of the University; the Regional Commissioner; and other dignitaries. Buglers of the Cambridgeshire Cadet Battalion blew a fanfare, and the crowd sang "O God our help in ages past". The sun blazed down and a few were overcome by emotion and the heat. Later there were patriotic music and displays by the Dagenham Girl Pipers, and the bands of the Home Guard and the Cadet Battalion toured the town. In the evening a torchlight procession ended with a beacon bonfire on Midsummer Common, and effigies of Hitler, Himmler and Goebbels were burned. The King broadcast at 9 pm and his address was relayed by loud-speakers to crowds in Market Square. To round off the day there was dancing by floodlight on Parker's Piece.

The pattern of events was much the same in Ipswich, where a crowd on the Cornhill heard the Prime Minister's broadcast and the Mayor's epilogue and sang the national anthem. The church bells rang, and later St Mary-le-Tower was packed to the doors, with the aisles crammed, for a service at which the Bishop of St Edmundsbury and Ipswich spoke sympathetically of those still held prisoner by the Japanese.

Most families, of course, celebrated in the absence of fathers and husbands. One Norwich lady described her VE-Day thus:

The torchlight procession and bonfire in Cambridge.   *Cambridge Daily News*

I had made flags for the children and sewed them to curtain rods. We hung them out of the children's bedroom window. We looked out all their red, white and blue clothes. Ann had a red, white and blue ribbon in her hair. Richard had a piece of ribbon on his cot. I had to have a ribbon in my hair, and the dolls and Daddy's photograph were also decked in ribbons . . . We had boiled eggs for breakfast as a treat. I listened to the wireless all day. Our next door neighbours on both sides were busy Spring-cleaning . . .

Later Richard and I caught the bus into the city. It wasn't very crowded. We passed a good many flags on the way, and one or two bonfires ready for the evening . . . I noticed that floodlights had been set up outside the main doors of the cathedral. I was told the Market Place was so full that buses had to be diverted . . .

My main feeling on V-Day was an intense loneliness. A day like that seems so unreal without one's husband. About 11 pm I turned the lights out and watched the searchlights in the sky. They were picking out planes which were flying across the sky like small silver birds, dropping Very lights. In the distance, I could hear people laughing and shouting, and see the lights of bonfires and hear continuous bangs . . .[3]

A Chelmsford hospital worker noted in his diary that the church bells were ringing and the nurses were wearing red, white and blue ribbons and rosettes. When he went off duty:

there was a bonfire outside the pub. Walking home I saw V-lights in some houses. In one place there was a bonfire on the grass verge by the roadside, a radio was blaring music, and people were dancing on the pavement. The local church was floodlit. The searchlights were interlacing in a marvellous moving pattern of light. I felt rather thrilled. We had come through.[4]

A misanthropic view of the proceedings is evident in the diary of a Bury St Edmunds woman who felt unwell and stayed in bed on VE-Day:

It's a nice warm day, but nowhere to go away from the celebrations. Fortunately, this is a back room and, thank the Lord, no flags are to be seen . . . Wish I could escape somewhere, but everywhere in England will be celebrating today . . . The bloody church bells have been ringing all the morning . . .

She was unable to maintain this mood against the tide of popular sentiment and later in the day she relented:

At 9.30 tonight several of us went along to the Angel Hill. Such a crowd, and the Angel Hotel illuminated with red, white and blue fairy lamps . . . . Dancing going on and all the children in the town dancing or in perambulators or on arms. Children and grownups dancing . . . In the Abbey gardens the fairy lights were very pretty among the greenery. The gardens were thronged with people . . .

A reminder of the hardships that accompanied victory came when her party looked for somewhere to eat, and entered a cafe . . .

Tea tasted rather awful and served in very thick, clumsy white cups and no saucers. Food was spam and potatoes, which I ordered. Then the girl returned to say "No potatoes", only spam sandwiches, so we had tea only . . . We felt life was unreal and we could not realise that the war with Germany was over . . .[5]

V-E DAY
SEETHING, ENGLAND
8 MAY 1945

At Felixstowe the band of the Gloucester Regiment marched through the town. In Colchester—where loud-speakers relayed music throughout the day and some buildings were floodlit—American and Canadian airmen and soldiers, French paratroopers, and British soldiers and sailors fraternized in the streets. At Great Yarmouth all craft on the river and at Felixstowe all ships in the harbour sounded their sirens. At Walton-on-the-Naze effigies of Hitler, Mussolini and Goering were burned.

Thus the day passed: bands playing, crowds dancing, bonfires burning. But many shared the sentiments contained in an address prepared by the chaplain at the USAAF base at Ridgwell and delivered at the service of thanksgiving there:

> Though it is a day of joy, it is not a day of triumph. It is one of grave responsibility. The war has come to an end but it has not been won. Whether we win the war will depend now on what we do from this point on. So far we have done only the ugly work. We have dug up the weeds, and I am glad to say have burned them. It now remains to plant the soil; to constructively remake the world; to make it a fit place to live, where we can laugh and where our children can sing and play.[6]

After station commanders on the US airfields had announced victory over Germany, there were services of thanksgiving and remembrance, with roll calls of colleagues who had died. The men were released from duty for the day, but they were restricted to the fields, guards were doubled to make sure that no one escaped, and all motor vehicles were grounded. The authorities did not risk letting the more boisterous types loose in the towns and the village pubs. Film shows ran all afternoon and evening, and at some bases free beer and whisky were available[7].

Members of thr 381st Bomb Group celebrate VE Day in the Non-Commissioned Officers Club at Ridgewell, 8th May, 1945. *Photo courtesy of Dave Osborne*

Sadly, the VE celebrations did not pass off without tragedy. Among the jostling crowds in St Benedict's Street, Norwich, a US army truck ran down and killed a ten-year-old girl; and in Gorleston a car containing three sailors from Lowestoft knocked down and killed a sixty-one-year-old Yarmouth woman.

On the following Sunday, 13th May, every town and village had its special religious service. Norwich cathedral overflowed and crowds in the Close heard the service over loud-speakers. The Bishop began with the words: "Lift up your hearts", but the burden of his sermon was what remained to be done. They had comrades in the Far East who must not be forgotten, and devastated Europe would have to be helped. "We must justify your preservation by the service we can render to a stricken world", he said. A USAAF band played for the hymn "Mine eyes have seen the glory of the coming of the Lord", music which many of the congregation probably knew better as "John Brown's body". After the service thousands of people lined the streets to watch a victory parade by about five thousand British and American troops, including five bands and uniformed members of the Civil Defence services.

65

They saw a spectacle never before witnessed in the city: the sun glinting on the bare steel of the fixed bayonets of the Royal Norfolk Regiment. Two months earlier, to mark "the affection of the citizens for their county regiment and admiration of the gallantry it had displayed over nearly three centuries", the City Council had conferred upon the regiment "the privilege, honour and distinction of marching through the city on all ceremonial occasions with bayonets fixed, colours flying and bands playing". This was the first occasion on which it exercised the new privilege. Every window overlooking the route and every accessible vantage point was occupied, and the crowds sent up great bursts of cheering, in turn for the Norfolk Regiment; for the Home Guard veterans; for the Indian soldiers recently returned from German prison camps; for the RAF; for girls of the ATS and the WAAF; and for the Civil Defence representatives. The salute was taken at the City Hall by Field Marshal Lord Ironside, the US General Leon Johnson, and the Lord Mayor, Mr E. F. Williamson.

On this same Sunday Rear-Admiral Karl Bruening brought to Felixstowe from Rotterdam two of the German E-boats which had operated from Dutch bases under his command. After the German navy had been driven from the English Channel, this E-boat force had fought doggedly to the end and had never quite been subdued. Now Admiral Bruening came to surrender his fleet and to hand over charts of German minefields in the North Sea. Two sleek grey E-boats made the passage at an impressive thirty-two knots, but they flew only tattered white flags.

About fifty miles off Felixstowe they were met by ten motor torpedo-boats of Coastal Forces from HMS *Beehive*. One of the naval officers who went aboard, Peter Scott, reported afterwards: "With some difficulty we persuaded the Germans to fall their crew in on deck as they entered harbour, where a great crowd of spectators was assembled on all the piers and jetties."[8] They made a spectacular entry to Felixstowe dock at relatively high speed, berthed alongside one of the escorting British boats, and an armed guard went on board. A special correspondent reported in the *Eastern Daily Press:*

> The German crews looked rather pleased about the whole proceedings. Rear Admiral Bruening did not look so happy. An insignificant-looking little man with a grim expression, he was piped over the side and on board the Admiral's barge, which was manned by Wrens.

The German admiral was received on *Beehive* by its Commanding Officer, Commander McCowan. The officers of the two E-boats were sent up to the Cliff Hotel at Felixstowe, then to a naval billet, and the crews were taken to Shotley in a motor launch. The Wrens rushed Admiral Bruening, in an admiral's barge, across the harbour to the flagship at Harwich for interrogation.

The services and parades on 13th May completed the official celebration of Victory in Europe, but many community events took place during the following week. Most towns and villages organized street tea-parties, as they had done at Coronation and Jubilee celebrations a few years earlier. Dozens of these open-air parties took place, and on more than one occasion a returning prisoner-of-war

Rear Admiral Karl Brauning steps aboard a barge manned by wrens to be taken to Harwich.

walked into his home street while one was in full swing[9].

A Chelmsford man noted in his diary:

Life is rapidly returning to what it was before VE day. The atmosphere of celebration has almost vanished. Few decorations remain. People realise that we shall not get back to normal for a long time. One of the roads adjoining ours had its victory celebration this evening. About fifteen Morrison table shelters were lined up along a short section of the road, which was beflagged. A bonfire with an effigy [presumably Hitler] was stacked in the middle of the road . . . At 10.45 p.m. the celebration was going strong. A powerful floodlight fixed on a tree lit up the road. Fireworks were being let off. A man was playing a piano on the path and people were dancing in the road. Many others were watching.[10]

At several US bases the British were invited to victory and/or farewell events. East Anglia received a royal visit – the Duchess of Kent toured Norwich, Cromer, Sheringham and King's Lynn and met among others the veteran lifeboatman and war hero Coxwain Henry Blogg.

Three months later victory in the Far East set off a new round of celebrations, and in East Anglia much greater emotion was generated on VJ-Day than had been the case in May. At last the men from Norfolk, Suffolk and Cambridgeshire would be coming home. There were more thanksgiving services and church bells pealing, more flags and fireworks, and—for the children—more sports and tea-parties.

A new Prime Minister, Clement Attlee, gave this victory broadcast. It came at midnight after many were in bed, but crowds were soon out in the streets. At Lowestoft ships' sirens woke sleepers when the news came through. In Thetford cars toured the town with their horns sounding. Elsewhere the bells were rung. In King's Lynn people appeared in pyjamas and dressing gowns to dance in the street. In Thetford a bonfire was lit of newspapers and old tyres in the market place, and it was 4 am before things began to quieten down. In Cromer street lights were switched on for the first time since 1939, and railway staff placed fog signals on the line for the early trains.

In Ipswich that night things did not go smoothly. The *East Anglian Daily Times* reported:

> In the early hours of yesterday the Cornhill was one mass of humanity ... Generally the people were in happy festive mood, but it was here in the earliest hours of the morning there came a black spot on the celebrations. A small section gave expression to excitable irresponsibility, which brought in its wake most foolish damage. The throwing of missiles began, and this destructive ebullition of spirits soon found the lower windows of the Town Hall and the Police Station wrecked, for no apparent cause ...

The damage was attributed to "some naval men and a few hooligan lads of about 15 to 18". In other parts of the town there were street parties, with dancing and singing to piano accordions. Bonfires were lit in many inappropriate places, and there was some destruction of property to feed the flames.

At Great Yarmouth, too, some of the crowd became over-excited and destructive. Just after midnight firemen were called to douse a bonfire that had got out of control in the forecourt of the Granville Hotel in Regent Road, but some of the crowd cut the hoses and attacked the firemen, injuring four of them. All night long excited crowds streamed along the Marine Parade, through the town's main streets and around the market place, not only dancing and singing but also committing a good deal of damage to property—windows were smashed and doors kicked in. Gorleston was also noisy during the night, until about 3 am.

Next day an orderly programme was carried through. In Great Yarmouth flags of the United Nations flew from tall flagpoles on the open space in front of the Town Hall. Crowds watched the ceremonial sheathing of the town's sword of justice, which had remained unsheathed since the outbreak of war. There was a similar sword-sheathing ceremony at Thetford.

At Lowestoft naval vessels in the Hamilton Dock displayed their flags and a Swedish four-master in port, the *Albatross*, joined in, with bunting from bowsprit to stern. The Royal Plain was encircled with flags and streamers and coloured lights, and it echoed with music all day. The Salvation Army band played hymns during the morning, and a dance band played popular tunes throughout the afternoon and evening. When an official bonfire was lit in the evening, a Japanese flag and effigy were on top.

At Woodbridge owners of cabin cruisers and motor boats took hundreds of youngsters for trips from Ferry Quay down the river. The Ipswich St John Ambulance Band provided music.

In Norwich within a few minutes of the Prime Minister's midnight broadcast people hurried from all parts of the city towards the market place, where they sang and danced in front of the City Hall. Servicemen, British and American, were prominent in the crowd, some in the slouch hats of the Burma campaign. Next day

The dense crowd in The Walk at Norwich during the afternoon of the first V.J. Day holiday.

Eastern Daily Press

the crowds were far greater than on VE-Day. A united service with civic leaders was held at St Peter Mancroft—where the bells were rung for several hours—and there was an evening service in the cathedral. On Tombland RAF officers and American GIs jitterbugged with Norwich lasses to music relayed from a dance in the Samson and Hercules House. The castle, the gates to the Close, the Guildhall and the City Hall tower were floodlit, and fireworks were let off and bonfires lit in different parts of the city.

One of the most carefully produced and impressive events was at Debenham, where more than two hundred torch bearers headed by the Town Band marched in procession through the village to Broad Meadow. There they formed a guard of honour on either side of a raised floodlit dais, on which stood a figure personifying liberty. Representatives of the armed forces and of all the wartime services marched to take their places on the dais, standing either side of Liberty. There was a minute's silence for the fallen, during which the lights were dimmed, to be refocused on a figure representing peace. The crowds sang, with the band, "Land of hope and glory", "Rule Britannia", and then "Abide with me"—during which flags of all the Allied nations were dipped—and then there was community singing.

Some places organized another VJ-Day on 17th September. In Ipswich, for example, there was a grand parade of all the Civil Defence services from Christchurch Park through the town. The former Regional Commissioner, Sir Will Spens, took the salute on Cornhill. In the afternoon a military band played in the park and the children paraded in fancy dress, and there was a friendly football match between Ipswich and Colchester at Portman Road.

The Princess Royal, Commandant-in-Chief of the British Red Cross Society, attended a regional thanksgiving service of the society on 14th October; it was attended by 2,500 people and held in Ely cathedral.

Cambridge University honoured the principal war leaders. Three of them, Mr John Winant, the US Ambassador in London; Admiral Lord Cunningham; and Marshal of the RAF Lord Portal, visited Cambridge on 29th November and each received the honorary degree of Doctor of Law. Others similarly honoured at a later date were Generals Eisenhower and Montgomery, Field Marshal Lord Alanbrooke, Field Marshal Sir Harold Alexander, and Marshal of the RAF Sir Arthur Tedder.

Amid the various celebrations the leader-writer of the *East Anglian Daily Times* offered a pretentious self-assessment: "We acknowledge the Divine grace

No other regiment equalled the Royal Norfolk's five war-time Victoria Crosses. These were the five VCs 1. Captain J. N. Randle (Kohima 1944) 2. Cpl S. Bates (Sourdeval 1944) 3. CSM G. Gristock (River Escout 1940) 4. Capt D. Jamieson (Orne Bridgehead 1944) 5. Lt G. A. Knowland (Kangau, Burma 1945).

Photo courtesy of Lt. Cmdr. P. K. Kemp

that has used us as instruments to bring about the downfall of evil regimes in the west and in the east." Many were less sensible of bestowal of grace than of exaction of pain. Each community now took a measure of its loss.

During five and a half years of war about five thousand tons of bombs had fallen on Norfolk, Suffolk, Essex, Cambridgeshire, Bedfordshire, Huntingdon-shire and the Isle of Ely; and official statistics showed that over one thousand people had been killed and over four thousand seriously injured. The total was made up of about 30,000 high explosive bombs, 575 parachute mines, 680 V-1 rockets, 429 V-2 rockets and about 160,000 incendiaries and other weapons. These figures do not include bombs on military property[11]. The War Damage Commission reported that there were 202,328 war-damaged properties in the Eastern Region at the end of the war.

The most heavily bombed town in the region was Great Yarmouth. Its Chief Constable, Mr C. G. Box, reported that there had been 219 raids, that 212 houses and 25 other properties had been destroyed, and that 1,427 houses and 172 other properties were so badly damaged that demolition was necessary.

Other statistics were[12]:

	No of alerts	"Crash" alarms	Killed	Injured
Norwich	1,530	130	340	1,092
Lowestoft	2,047	628	266	690
Great Yarmouth	2,044	1,854	217	588
Ipswich	–	–	73	412
Colchester	1,094	–	54	100
Cambridge	329	–	39	71
Clacton, Walton and Frinton	–	–	37	–

Some communities had been relatively fortunate. At Brightlingsea, for example, despite 917 alerts and 1,544 bombs there had been only nineteen casualties, including only two killed. In 115 parishes of the Cambridgeshire rural area there had been 1,634 high explosive bombs, seven parachute mines, 221 anti-personnel bombs, six phosphorus bombs and at least seven thousand incendiaries, yet only three civilians had been killed and about twenty five injured. West Mersea had had sixty-three high explosive bombs and 204 incendiaries, but no-one had been killed and only eight injured.

Bombs had not been the only hazard. In Norfolk alone during the course of the war twenty German planes had been brought down and 933 Allied aircraft had crashed—677 RAF and 256 USAAF.

Representative of losses suffered by the East Anglian regiments was the 1st Battalion of the Royal Norfolk Regiment. Between D-Day and VE-Day it lost 250 men killed, of its war establishment of 845 officers and men. The 2nd Battalion of the Essex Regiment lost 156 of a war establishment of 799.

CHAPTER SIX

"Revolution by Consent"

T HE END of the wartime coalition government and the prospect of an early general election came on to the agenda from the earliest days of 1945. The administrative arrangements for a poll had already been made, and it was announced during January that electors on active service overseas would be able to vote. The count would be delayed for nineteen days to allow their voting papers to be collected and flown back to the United Kingdom. Counting would take two days, so that there would be a three-week interval between polling day and the declaration of results.

Winston Churchill addressed a Conservative Party conference in London in mid-March and anticipated the election. He said:

> This Parliament is nearly ten years old. Executive government must refresh itself by direct contact with the electors. Should the war in Europe end before the summer ends, or even sooner, as it might well do, war conditions will no longer prevent the holding of a general election.

He regretted that the Labour and Liberal Parties intended to "resume their full liberty of action and thus bring their famous coalition to an end".

There had been no general election in Britain since 1935, and so no one under the age of thirty-one had ever voted. In these circumstances no one felt confident about the outcome of a poll in the new post-war world. During the nineteen-thirties Labour had suffered two overwhelming election defeats, and the Conservatives had had a majority of more than two to one in the Commons. They had been in power for eighteen of the twenty-one inter-war years. And now they had Churchill, the great wartime leader, at their head.

A by-election in Chelmsford in January 1945 suggested a profound change of public opinion during the war years. The new left-of-centre Common Wealth Party had challenged the electoral truce and had secured three seats in the Commons. It now fielded a candidate in Chelmsford, twenty-eight-year-old Wing Commander E. R. Millington, who had led a squadron of Lancasters in many bombing raids on Germany. His Coalition Conservative opponent was also an RAF officer: Flight Lieutenant Brian Cook. This was the first by-election to be fought on a new register, increased by thirteen thousand since the previous general election and now including proxy votes on behalf of servicemen and women overseas and votes by repatriated prisoners-of-war.

Millington's meetings were well attended, and there was a sixty-nine per cent poll, which was high for a wartime by-election. The 16,624 Conservative majority was overturned and the Common Wealth man emerged as victor with a majority of 6,431. This was the third successive defeat for the government in by-elections, and Millington declared "It shows that the people are tired of the old order and want a new plan." The *East Anglian Daily Times* in a leading article suggested that a majority of the Chelmsford electorate had shown itself ready "to hand over their destinies to a revolutionary change of regime", and went on to comment:

> All we need remark about that regime is the one undeniable fact that, however good its intentions, however ethical its aims, the citizen would find himself in a bondage which conflicts with his most fundamental instinct as a Britisher and little different from the one which for five weary years he has made heavy sacrifices in destroying . . . Those who imagine the New Jerusalem to depend for its architecture on state control and management of everything and everybody, from the moment they are born to the moment they are enshrouded for final departure to an even better world, have learned nothing from the fate of Italy and Germany.

The scene was set for a hard-hitting contest as the parties began to tune up their constituency machines for the election ahead. A few sitting Members of Parliament announced that they would not seek re-election, including Mr J. A. Christie in South Norfolk and Lord Fermoy at King's Lynn. Whenever they could the parties adopted prospective candidates with local roots. Thus Mr Edwin Gooch, well known in the eastern counties as a national leader of the Agricultural Workers' Union, was adopted by Labour for North Norfolk; Mr Christopher Mayhew, a scion of an old Norfolk family who was a major in the army "somewhere in Germany", became Labour candidate for South Norfolk; and a Cambridge man who was serving in Italy, Major Arthur Leslie Symonds, M.A., was the only nominee to represent Labour in the contest in his native town. A Norwich footwear manufacturer, Lieutenant L. E. Goodman, who was serving in the RASC, was selected as the standard bearer for the Cambridge Liberals.

Because the Conservatives selected an "outsider" as their candidate for South Norfolk, an Independent Conservative candidate—Major John Holt Wilson—took the field and an Independent Conservative Association was formed in the constituency. Major Wilson owned and farmed the Redgrave Estate, while his Tory opponent, Colonel J. Sandeman Allen, was dismissed as "a city man who has no knowledge of agriculture".

All the candidates, full of optimism about their prospects, adopted gladiatorial poses and promised energetic action when the gun was fired. Mayhew, for example, announced that he would address eighty-two public meetings and, in a message to his divisional Labour Party, declared: "There is a tide running in the electorate, soldiers and civilians alike, in favour of new ideas and new men to put them through . . . Millions of plain folk will vote Labour this time who have never done so before."

On the national scene bickering broke out in April between coalition partners. Ernest Bevin and Brendan Bracken clashed in public and an *Eastern Daily Press* headline declared that the parties were "Clearing the Decks for the Election Fight".

Hobart Road, Cambridge decorated for the return of prisoners of war.　*Cambridge Local History Library*

Churchill recognized the Bevin–Bracken exchange as evidence that the coalition must soon break up and acted accordingly. On the evening that news reached him that Hitler had committed suicide, Churchill went into conclave with his Conservative Party chiefs about their strategy for the election.

The Labour Party conference, in private session in Blackpool on 21st May rejected a proposal by Churchill that the coalition should continue until VJ-Day. The Prime Minister then visited the King and offered his resignation, and within four days he formed a caretaker Conservative government. It was announced that Parliament would be dissolved on 15th June. One of the two Norwich MPs, Sir Geoffrey Shakespeare, was made a privy councillor in the Dissolution Honours.

The Conservative Party manifesto promised:

the fullest opportunity for individual initiative and the removal of wartime controls as the necessity for them disappears . . . a determined policy for full employment and a rising standard of living . . . a prosperous and healthy agriculture . . . an all-out drive for more and better houses . . . the removal of need from the home, by carrying out complete schemes of national insurance and family allowances, and improved health and hospital services, and an educational system giving equal opportunities for all.

Churchill opened the Conservative campaign proper with a broadcast on 4th June in which he echoed the view of the *East Anglian Daily Times* in its leading article a few months earlier: "I declare to you from the bottom of my heart that no

Socialist system can be established without a political police . . . They would have to fall back on some form of Gestapo". Elaborating on this theme, he suggested that everyone would be told where they had to work, where they could go and what they could say, what views they might hold and within what limits they might express them, where their wives were to go to queue for the state ration, and what education their children should receive to mould their views of human liberty and conduct. The *East Anglian Daily Times* pursued the argument with enthusiasm: "The perfectly plain single issue in this general election is for our people to decide whether individual freedom is to continue and survive, or each and every individual is to live as a state automaton".

Most of the national newspapers supported the Conservatives and used more extravagant language. For example, the *Daily Express*, which claimed the largest circulation of any paper in the world, published a leading article asserting: "The Socialist Party is a many-headed monster . . . But there is one notion in every head. And that is: socialist revolution, even it if means the wholesale slaughter of the ancient rights and liberties of the people."

The Labour leader, Clement Attlee, broadcast twenty-four hours after Churchill. He ignored the Gestapo allegations, concentrating on Labour's conviction that it was necessary to mobilize the resources of the nation for peace, in the same way as the coalition government had mobilized them for war. He challenged the Conservative belief that the interest of all would somehow be served if every individual pursued his or her own interest. Experience had shown no evidence of that, he insisted. In the past, freedom for the rich had involved slavery for the poor.

Labour had the support of the *Daily Mirror*, which listed the four vital election issues as housing, full employment, social security and international co-operation. It conceded that all parties professed to believe in these things, and argued that the sincerity of their belief should be gauged by reference to their past record.

There was a big row in the Commons on 12th June as to whether servicemen and women should be allowed to take part in the campaign while in uniform. It was eventually agreed that candidates should not appear in uniform, but that men and women in uniform would be free to put questions at public meetings.

A few national figures visited East Anglia during the course of the campaign. When Ernest Bevin went to Cambridge to speak in support of the borough and county Labour candidates, there was a queue all round the Guildhall; he spoke from the balcony to the large crowd which was unable to fit into the hall.

Three days before the poll Churchill, in another broadcast, addressed a special message to the forces. He told them he would not be prepared to serve in a Labour government, and added: "There is no truth in stories now being put about that you can vote for my political opponents, whether they be Labour or Liberal, without at the same time voting for my dismissal from power."

The following day Herbert Morrison responded to this challenge at a meeting in the Theatre Royal in Norwich: "No government could win a war on its own, let alone one man in the government . . . It was the people who won the war and you are going to decide next Thursday whether the people are going to win the peace . . .".

The *Eastern Daily Press* in a leading article on the eve of poll, adopted a generally pro-Conservative line and expressed the view that the chance of Labour obtaining a clear majority was "pretty remote". The author evidently did not have his ear sufficiently close to the ground, for there was much evidence to suggest that change was coming. In Bury St Edmunds, a town which had always shown solid Conservative sympathies, one resident noted in her diary a month before polling day:

> The British Restaurant was funny today . . . The cashier had a red ribbon on her coat and a red blouse. The cook's blouse was red, and her hair had a red ribbon. A server had a red blouse, and a red cord pinned on her costume coat. Around the room were other red blouses, coats and hair ribbons . . . I will wear a red blouse tomorrow, as I hope to go round inducing old ladies to enter a car and vote . . . Bury is infinitely more "red" than one ever would have supposed . . . [1]

Another diarist, living in Chelmsford, noted: "Mr C. said he thought the Tories would just get in on the strength of Churchill's popularity, but, he said, 'Churchill's popularity will wane'."[2]

Polling was on Thursday, 5th July, a fine though dull day in most of the region. Polling booths were erected in all the army and RAF camps; later there were complaints that service voters in some of them did not receive their ballot papers—at the Rivenhall base, for example, they were twenty per cent short[3].

The results were declared on 26th July. The *Cambridge Daily News* frontpage lead that day was headlined:

LABOUR GOVT. RETURNED

Sweeping Gains in all Parts

MANY MINISTERS DEFEATED

The story below referred to "the most astonishing and significant British election of the century". Out of a total of 640 seats in Parliament, Labour had a majority of 202 over the Conservatives and of 158 over all the other parties combined. Next morning the *Eastern Daily Press* summed up: "For the first time in the electoral history of Norfolk, not a single Conservative Member will sit in the new Parliament." Its front-page headline was:

ATTLEE CHOOSING HIS CABINET

Mr Churchill says Farewell

On inside pages there was the news of "Labour's sweeping victory in Norfolk":

> Labour almost swept the decks in local constituencies . . . There appears to have been a fairly high percentage of polling—approximate figures are Norwich 75 per cent, Yarmouth 69 per cent, Lynn 71 per cent, South Norfolk 58 per cent, North Norfolk 70 per cent, East Norfolk 68 per cent, South West Norfolk 66 per cent and Lowestoft 67 per cent.

Norfolk proved to be typical of the region as a whole—indeed of the nation. In the big urban constituencies—Norwich, Cambridge, Peterborough, King's Lynn, Great Yarmouth, Lowestoft and Colchester—Churchill's men were thrust aside and Labour was triumphant. In the rural constituencies it was much the same story: Cambridgeshire, North Norfolk, South Norfolk, South-West Norfolk and the Suffolk countryside around Sudbury switched allegiance from the Conservative to the Labour Party. Only in Bury St Edmunds, Woodbridge and Saffron Walden did the Conservatives hold on, with greatly reduced majorities; and they gained a seat in the Isle of Ely at the expense of the Liberals. Liberal National candidates, who were reliable allies of the Conservatives, retained the constituencies of East Norfolk, Harwich and Huntingdonshire. Wing Commander Millington held on to the Chelmsford seat he had won for the Common Wealth Party a few months earlier.

In the eastern counties the first results were announced at about 10.30 am. At Great Yarmouth fewer than a hundred people were present to hear the declaration that Squadron Leader E. Kinghorn, the Labour man, had displaced Mr P. W. Jewson, who had been the Conservative MP for the constituency for four years—but as soon as the figures were posted outside the Town Hall a big crowd rapidly assembled. Soon the Hall Quay and Regent Street junction was impassable.

Then came the South Norfolk and East Norfolk results, declared by the High Sheriff of Norfolk at Norwich Shirehall. In South Norfolk the election had been complicated by the intervention of the unofficial Tory, but the Labour man, Major Christopher Mayhew, took over the seat with a clear majority over both Conservative candidates combined.

Meanwhile at Aylsham Town Hall the North Norfolk result showed another Labour nominee, Mr Edwin Gooch, displacing Sir Thomas Cook, who had been the Conservative Member since 1935.

In Cambridge the Mayor emerged from the Guildhall at 11.30 am to announce to a crowd of several hundred that Lieutenant Commander Richard Tufnell, the Conservative, had lost the seat he had held since 1934. The new Labour MP was Major A. L. Symonds.

Half an hour later the High Sheriff of Norfolk came on to the balcony of the Norwich City Hall to announce to a crowd of a few hundred that the government had lost both the city seats, Lady Noel-Buxton and Mr John Paton replacing Sir Geoffrey Shakespeare (Member for sixteen years) and Mr Henry Strauss (Member for ten years). Labour supporters were wild with enthusiasm.

HOW EAST ANGLIAN VOTERS SWUNG LEFT IN 1945

KEY:

Labour constituencies

Conservative constituencies

Liberal constituency

Common Wealth constituency

Cambridge Borough was a Labour gain
Cambridge University elected one Conservative
   and one Independent (previously
   two Conservatives)
Norwich - Labour gained two seats
Ipswich - Labour retained seat
Eye - M.P. sitting as Independent fought as Liberal

GAINS are shown CAMBRIDGE   **SEATS RETAINED** are shown HARWICH

Labour's success in holding Ipswich was also announced, by the Ipswich Mayor, at about noon. Despite the change of representation there was very little excitement when the results were announced at Sudbury and Lowestoft.

By the evening there was widespread Labour celebration throughout the region. In Cambridge about three thousand people gathered on Parker's Piece for a Labour victory rally addressed by the new town and county MPs. In Great Yarmouth the new Member was feted at a rally in the Market Square. Elsewhere — as in North Norfolk, where Mr Edwin Gooch met his supporters at the Cromer Labour Club — there were quieter but no less happy gatherings.

There was one other constituency in the region, for which the results were not known until four days later. Cambridge University had its own direct representation in the House of Commons, electing two MPs by proportional representation with voting by post. Mr J. B. Priestley, the novelist–playwright who had gained a big reputation as a wartime broadcaster, had entered the ring as an Independent Progressive candidate. The count took place on 30th July in the Senate House. Mr Kenneth Pickthorn, standing as a Conservative, quickly emerged as one victor, his 10,202 votes in the first ballot being sufficient to ensure his election. Three more counts were required, however, to decide who should have the second seat. At the first count the other candidates had secured the following votes: Priestley (Independent Progressive) 5,041; H. Wilson Harris (Independent) 3,574; Dr Charles Hill (Independent) 2,238; and Air Commodore E. L. Howard-Williams (Independent) 1,036. Hill and Howard-Williams lost their deposits. After transfer of votes the final result was Pickthorn 7,364, Harris 6,556, and Priestley 5,745.

General election headlines from Friday, 27th July's, East Anglian Daily Times.

IPSWICH, FRIDAY, JULY 27, 1945

Mr. ATTLEE PREMIER AFTER GREAT ELECTION LANDSLIDE

LABOUR SWEEPS THE COUNTRY, AND SECURES 390 SEATS

CHURCHILL'S GOOD-BYE MESSAGE : RETURN TO POTSDAM UNCERTAIN

REASONS FOR COUNTRY'S REJECTION OF CONSERVATIVES

Mr. C. R. Attlee became Prime Minister last night shortly after Mr. Churchill had handed his resignation to the King at Buckingham Palace as a dramatic sequel to Britain's amazing General Election swing-over to Labour.

When the last of the day's declarations was announced, Labour had 390 seats, against the Conservatives' 195 and Liberals' 11.

THE FINAL STATE OF PARTIES LAST NIGHT WAS:

A remarkable feature of the campaign was the universal acknowledgement that it had been fought without rancour. Defeated Sir Geoffrey Shakespeare told the Norwich crowd: "I have no complaints. This has been a very fair fight." His Conservative colleague, Mr Henry Strauss, concurred — "Democracy has spoken." In King's Lynn the Conservative candidate acknowledged that there had been "absolutely fair play and it has been a most enjoyable and interesting fight". In South Norfolk Mr Holt Wilson congratulated the victorious Labour man on "a magnificent clean fight". In East Norfolk, where Brigadier Frank Medlicott held the seat, he spoke of a "very clean and straightforward campaign"; and in Lowestoft the Tory standard-bearer spoke of "a straight clean fight".

Only a single incident in Ipswich marred this picture. The Conservative candidate complained to Mr Richard Stokes, the Labour victor, that a party of two hundred youths had stuck Labour bills on, and thrown stones at, his agent's car.

The *Eastern Daily Press* summed up:

> Nowhere, we think in the whole of Norfolk, has there been any incident of any lasting significance that can leave the slightest sense of personal rancour. The whole campaign has been happily free of either political or personal bitterness.

Although the regional press in its opinion columns had almost unanimously supported the Conservative candidates, it had conscientiously reported the speeches of all candidates throughout the campaign. The *East Anglian Daily Times* in particular was a model of fair and full political coverage. J. F. Wright, the Norfolk farmers' spokesman, later wrote in his regular column in the *Eastern Daily Press:*

> Three of the new M. Ps will enter Parliament with a wide knowledge of agriculture and that must be taken into account as a compensating factor [Messrs Wise, Gooch and Dye]. Those of us who are not of the Socialist political persuasion will not withhold our best wishes from those whose responsibility it now is to see that agriculture continues to receive a just reward.

A retired Norwich school-teacher who had returned to Norwich from Dorset to cast her vote commented on the result:

> Surprise, with a sort of shock, at Labour's triumph. At first a feeling of apprehension. I voted Labour in Norwich with the intention of helping to lessen the Tory majority. I wouldn't have minded Tories in at present, with a much smaller majority, so that opposition could be effective . . . Now I am interested and not unhopeful about what Labour will do . . . [4]

An American observer who was serving in the USAAF in East Anglia noted:

> The most encouraging sign I found of England's enduring strength was the wave of hope and exultation which swept over the country when Labour came into power, and in the enthusiastic willingness of a people exhausted by six years of war and almost bankrupt as a nation to launch on a revolution by consent . . . The natural tendency would have been to relax, to rest on one's oars, to drop all controls, and to try to return to pre-war "normal" as soon as possible. Instead, the people put into power a Government pledged to continued controls, to almost indefinite austerity in living standards, and to a gradual transformation of the national economy.[5]

Some greeted the results with sour disapproval. When the new Cambridge Labour Member spoke at a meeting of the University Socialist Society at St John's College on 29th July a political opponent ignited a smoke canister in the hall and four people suffering from fumes needed hospital treatment. The meeting continued in another room.

A correspondent wrote to the *East Anglian Daily Times* complaining that all Suffolk MPs elected in the general election had been returned on minority votes. The Conservatives had polled more votes in the aggregate than had either of the other parties, yet they only held one-third of the seats. In the county as a whole it had taken 44,000 votes to elect a Liberal, 40,000 to elect a Conservative, but only 26,000 to elect a Labour MP. Another correspondent responded that in the previous municipal elections in Ipswich Labour had polled most votes but the Conservatives had won the majority of the seats.

At the municipal elections in November 1945 many of the councillors retiring from the local councils had been elected in 1936. They would normally have retired in 1939. Others had been co-opted during the war years, when there was a party truce. The results confirmed the swing to the left.

Labour gained twelve seats on the Town Council in Great Yarmouth, eleven in Ipswich, eight in Lowestoft, five in Norwich, five in Cambridge, and two in King's Lynn. In Norwich all fifteen Labour candidates were elected, strengthening the party's control of the city council, where the party strengths now became: Labour 38, Independent Labour 4, Conservative 18, Liberal 3, Independent 1. In Ipswich twenty-three seats were contested; Labour increased its share of them from three to fourteen and became the largest group on the Town Council, but it just failed to secure an overall majority. In Cambridge Labour increased its share of the nineteen seats to be filled from four to nine, and Conservatives lost their overall control but remained the largest party. At Colchester Labour took control. In Lowestoft the Conservatives retained effective control, but were dependent upon the support of three Independents.

After the elections came the selection of Mayors. Mr Sidney Albert Bailey, twenty-three years a city councillor, was Labour's choice as Lord Mayor of Norwich. Chelmsford, Great Yarmouth and King's Lynn were among the towns that elected a Labour Mayor for the first time. For only the third time in its history Cambridge Council elected a woman Mayor—Lady Bragg, who represented Newnham. Wife of a distinguished scientist, Sir Lawrence Bragg, she had been WVS central organiser during the war.

In Lowestoft some councillors had met privately more than a month before the local government poll and had decided they would invite Major S. W. Humphery to continue in office. He had been Mayor for thirteen years, including the whole period of the war. After the election and sweeping Labour gains the matter was put to a vote of the new council, and it elected a Labour nominee, Mr J. W. Woodrow. Humphery resigned his aldermancy on the spot and walked out.

CHAPTER SEVEN

Multitudes On The Move

WHEN THE war in Europe ended the one thought in every mind was of home and of how to get there as quickly as possible. Some unfortunate people had no homes to which they could return; there were hundreds—possibly thousands—of them in East Anglia, but literally millions elsewhere in Europe.

Those who had been evacuated from their homes and schools in the restricted coastal areas of Norfolk, Suffolk and Essex were first on the move. School-children returning to their mothers in London after spending the war in East Anglia were next. Then came the exodus of the American servicemen making for the United States and the complementary movement of liberated prisoners-of-war to their own countries. Finally—in a never-ending and uncountable stream of human flotsam—there were the former internees of concentration and prison camps, slave-labourers and displaced persons, and Germans expelled from eastern Europe or uprooted from their native habitation.

The Ministry of Health announced at the end of March that help was available to families wishing to return to homes in Great Yarmouth, Lowestoft, Aldeburgh, Southwold, Felixstowe, Leiston, Southend, Colchester, Harwich, Brightlingsea and Clacton. It advised, however, against a general rush back and said that unaccompanied children who had been evacuated under official schemes should in no circumstances return. Six weeks later, with the fighting over in Europe, it gave an all-clear signal and offered free travel vouchers to adults and to children accompanying their mothers. Special trains or coaches were arranged for unaccompanied children. There was one proviso: only those whose homes had survived the coastal bombing qualified for assistance.

A few well-to-do parents had sent their children to live with families in the United States and Canada for the duration of the war, and these privileged youngsters now returned to their parents—there were five Norwich children in parties which returned from Canada in mid-August. Most fee-paying schools in the region had been evacuated to safer areas of Britain, and they now began to return. Gresham School returned to Holt from Newquay, and the Leys School to Cambridge from the Atholl Palace Hotel in Pitlochry, Scotland.

Many children had been evacuated *into* East Anglia from London and its suburbs, and on 2nd May the Minister of Health circulated a plan for "Operation London Return" to all local authorities, again with the proviso that only those with homes to go to should travel. Others were to stay put. It took about a month to organise the special trains and buses—and the farewell parties. When these

B-17's lined up at Ridgewell, ready to leave for home, at the end of the war in Europe, May 1945.
Photo courtesy of Dave Osborne

children had first arrived with their foster parents there had often been acute social problems and serious tensions. Now, with the moment of parting approaching, there came awareness of deep emotional attachments developed during the war.

Typical of many community leaders, the Mayor of Beccles, Rear Admiral C. S. Johnson, gave a farewell party for evacuees who had attended schools in his borough. The Mayor of Romford came to express thanks for hospitality given and to lead his children back to their home town. This party was a genuine community effort: the WVS served tea and the RAF provided entertainment. When the children boarded the train for London there were tears on both sides. According to reports in the local press, "considerable emotion" was shown at similar gatherings in many other towns and villages.

The easy-going folk of the eastern counties had learned a lot about the get-up-and-go characteristics of their American visitors, but still they were astonished at the speed with which the US servicemen and women made for home once hostilities in Europe had ended. Within a week of the German surrender the first USAAF bomb groups were beginning to leave. Within a few months forty thousand flew home in the bombers, twenty men in each; planes took off almost daily, flying via the Azores. Most of the ground crewmen went home in the *Queen*

Mary, the *Queen Elizabeth* and other liners; eventually 370 ships were used to ferry them and an average of three thousand men a day arrived in New York.

By the end of June Liberator B-24 bomb groups had left Bungay, Hethel, Old Buckenham, Shipdham and Wendling; and Flying Fortress B-17 bomb groups had vacated Alconbury, Bassingbourn, Deenethorpe, Ridgewell, Nuthampstead and Glatton. By the end of July the B-24s had left Attlebridge, Horsham St Faith and Seething; and other B-24 bomb groups were lined up and scheduled for immediate departure from Flixton, Hardwick, North Pickenham, Tibenham and Rackheath.

Most of the remaining Fortresses left in August: from Deopham Green, Eye, Framlingham, Horham, Rattlesden and Sudbury. Except at Rougham, Snetterton and Thorpe Abbots—where they stayed until the end of the year—the Fortresses had all departed by early September. USAAF fighter squadrons, too, departed within weeks of the armistice, apart from those at Bodney, East Wretham, Fowlmere and Honington, which were not vacated until October or November.

East Anglians thronged the streets to watch the Americans march away to waiting trucks and railway stations *en route* to the ports. At many of the bases the bombers circled the field in a final farewell gesture. Some USAAF units left monuments of their stay. Saffron Walden Town Council accepted a gift of £4,500 from a fighter wing towards the cost of a recreation and sports ground; it was to be the wing's memorial to comrades who had died and tribute to the people of Saffron Walden. The 392nd Bomb Group at Wendling constructed a marble obelisk.

Before the partings there were many expressions of mutual admiration. Lieutenant General James Doolittle, Commander of the US 8th Air Force, said in London on 11th May:

> At every one of our bomber bases the British people have been real friends to us. Although there have been a lot of jokes about the boys here, I am quite sure the British people are going to feel the same regret at losing the boys.

American airmen present the Mayor of Colchester (Ald. A. W. Piper) with a piece of plate before their departure, July 1945.
Photo courtesy of Mrs Hervey Benham

The following day King George and Queen Elizabeth visited 8th Air Force headquarters at High Wycombe and the King pronounced Doolittle an Honorary Knight Commander of the Bath.

The *Eastern Daily Press* published a letter to the editor from "A Yank in Norfolk", who wrote:

> In the years to come, wherever the men of the Division meet, there will be the fondest of memories and reminiscences of happy hours spent in Norwich and its environs. We sincerely hope that the overall impression we leave with you is, at least, kindred to the one we take with us. It has been a privilege to dwell among you . . .

On 2nd August the Freedom of Cambridge was conferred on the three hundred thousand men of the 8th USAAF at a ceremony in the Market Square, which was decked with flags and banners and packed with crowds. The Mayor presented an oak casket containing the scroll to Major General William E. Kepner, Commanding Officer of the 8th; he in turn presented the Mayor with an 8th Air Force shield to be hung in the Guildhall. The large crowd was entertained by massed American and RAF bands.

The Mayor said:

> Throughout our countryside and in this town—their chief leave town—the Americans have endeared themselves to us by their heroism, their understanding, their keen interest in our

Major General William E. Kepner receives the freedom of Norwich in the Council Chamber.

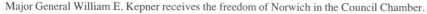

Eastern Daily Press

ways and doings, their great generosity and, above all perhaps, the great love they have shown to our children. You will be kindly spoken of by generations of Cambridge folk, and we hope you will take away with you nothing but kindly thoughts of Cambridge.

Then, more poignantly, he said it had been Cambridge's privilege to provide a site for the last resting place of those of the force who had died in the cause of freedom.

The wives, parents and other relatives of those who did not return may in time find some comfort in knowing that this cemetery is situated upon what we consider to be the most beautiful hill in the neighbourhood of Cambridge. The country visible is undulating and well-wooded, and is famed in our town for being a haunt of nightingales ...

There was a garden party for the Americans in the grounds of Pembroke College, and in the evening more than ten thousand people gathered on Parker's Piece to celebrate the event—a larger crowd than on VE-Day. Again there was dancing and fireworks, and on this occasion also an exhibition baseball match.

In October, at a ceremony in the Guildhall, the 8th Air Force presented Cambridge with the instrument panel of the last Fortress to bomb Europe, *Angel Swamp* of 384th Bomb Group. It had flown from Grafton to bomb the Skoda armaments works at Pilsen at 11.16 am on 25th April.

Norwich City Council conferred the honorary Freedom of Norwich on Major General William E. Kepner, commanding general of the US 8th Air Force—the first time this gesture had been made to a foreigner. The Mayor of Ipswich presented an illuminated scroll to Brigadier General E. L. Eubank, general officer commanding the 3rd Air Division, US Army, at a ceremony at Portman Road. Smaller communities made their own tributes in various ways. The chairman of the Loddon Rural District Council, Miss J. Carr, thanking the USAAF representative from nearby Seething, presented him with a framed embroidered map of England which was an old heirloom of her family.

The twenty-eighth birthday anniversary of the 8th Air Force fell on 1st August, and on that day fifteen American bases in East Anglia were opened to the public for the first time. Most of the bases put on a display of formation flying by Fortresses and Mustangs, and many visitors squeezed their way into bombers lined up on the ground. Over seven thousand people went to the Martlesham base.

The sweetness of these relations was soured briefly when rumours circulated that there had been wanton destruction of food and clothing on the USAAF bases being evacuated. The *Eastern Daily Press* investigated and concluded that the Americans were "exercising the utmost care to avoid preventable waste". This was not quite a complete denial and later in the year the evidence of deliberate destruction became irrefutable. When a Rackheath man who had visited the local US base daily to supply newspapers was fined twenty pounds in September for being in unlawful possession of army stores, he told the magistrates at Taverham that "when the men left, the stores left behind were burnt up, including cycles, boots and flying coats. There was a heap of goods and a bonfire to dispose of it ...".

During October there were several similar prosecutions in Norfolk. Dereham magistrates dismissed two such cases after a stoker employed at the Wendling base gave evidence that he had burned good clothes and equipment in the furnaces, including tins of food. The Air Ministry clerk of works at Wendling, also called as a witness, said the Americans had packed up what material and equipment they wanted. Other things had been put in bins and later dumped. Asked if any civilians went to the dumps, he replied: "It was like a cattle market. People went there with perambulators and with high-powered motorcars and filled them up from the dumps."

A Bury St Edmunds woman gave this account of what she had seen at Great Ashfield:

> The Americans left in a blaze of ill-feeling. When they were packing up to go all food, canned as well as fresh, the entire PX stores, everything there was, was taken in lorry loads and dumped in the middle of the airfield and burnt . . . A lot of people tried to get some of this and were fired on. It went on every day for three weeks . . . The same happened to hundreds of bikes, they were piled into a tremendous heap and tracked vehicles ran over them to smash them up . . . [1]

Before they left for home many of the American ground crews were flown on "trolley missions" over Germany to see its shattered cities, and over parts of Great Britain to see something of the country they had been defending. One of these flights ended in disaster. The Reverend James Good Brown noted in his diary at Ridgewell.

> An excursion flight was planned for Ireland . . . Each outfit on the base picked out its man for the trip, the one who was thought to be the most deserving . . . Thirty-one men were picked to spend a week in Belfast . . . [2]

The plane hit the peak of the two-thousand-foot mountain on the Isle of Man and none of the thirty-one—who included the crew—survived.

On 25th April, 1945 a USAAF furlough flight to Northern Ireland ended in disaster. Over 30 airmen on their way to attend a Roosevelt Memorial Service crashed into a mountainside. The picture shows the bodies awaiting flight back to Ridgewell. *Photo courtesy of Dave Osborne*

The first G.I. brides sailing from Southampton for America on the S.S. *Argentina*. *Planet News*

At the end of the European war each bomb group made a tally like this example:

> The 381st flew a total of 297 missions in combat, hitting every important target on the Continent. They hit Berlin and vicinity twenty times. The Group is credited with knocking down 223 enemy fighters and dropping more than 22,000 tons of bombs."[3]

There were other counts to be made. GIs in Britain had fathered about seventy thousand of the three hundred thousand illegitimate babies born during the war years (three times the pre-war rate).

More happily, East Anglia had produced a high proportion of the fifty thousand British girls the Americans had taken as brides. A few of them, who had been married for some time, emigrated to their new homes in the United States before VE-Day on troopships that were returning otherwise empty. The others were impatient to follow.

A GI brides club was formed in Norfolk in August when about two hundred of the brides—and some of their babies—attended a gathering at the Bishop's Palace in Norwich at the invitation of the American Red Cross. Their average age was twenty. The officials of the ARC told the girls bluntly that they could give them no idea when they might be able to join their husbands in the USA, adding:

> Some of you might have to wait till next spring and even the autumn, but while you are still in Norfolk we hope the club will be a means of bringing together brides whose future homes will be in the same state.

Each woman received a copy of *The Brides' Guide to the US*, issued by the US Office of War Information in London, which told them: "We want you to learn to sing 'The Star Spangled Banner' and 'God Bless America'.

This advice reinforced guidance that had been offered at an earlier gathering at the Bull hotel in Cambridge by Mrs Quincy Wright, a leading figure in the National League of Women Voters in the United States. She briefed a gathering of GI brides on American customs, beginning gently with the elementary rules such as coffee and fruit juice at breakfast and then imparting this more serious information:

> The great idea of an American wife is to "get through" the housework and do something else. If she takes all day to do her work she is not considered so efficient as she should be. When she has finished she does what she wants to do—shopping for clothes, visiting, or studying, for instance—always coming home in time to cook the dinner for her husband for about six o'clock in the evening. The dinner is very important, and when her husband arrives a woman is expected to look very beautiful and very fresh, as though she had done nothing all day . . . Wives of Americans must become used to the idea of a budget, allotting so much for rent, food, clothes and a car.

By the autumn of 1945 the popular press had produced a new name for these women—they called them "GI wallflowers"—and this did nothing to ease their restlessness. Two hundred of them demonstrated in London, waving "Forgotten GI Wives" banners and chanting "We want a boat"*. The Cambridge Wives Club disapproved of this militancy and withheld its support; it thought public sympathy might be alienated by the use of children and babies in the protest parade, and it preferred that a petition should be organized and presented to the US Embassy. On the last day of the year the front page of the *Eastern Daily Press* reported that 26,866 of the brides had been "processed" and the first 1,200 would embark towards the end of January 1946.

Not every GI bride reached America, for some of the marriages did not endure. In the Divorce Court in London in June a USAAF sergeant was granted a divorce from a wife he had married in Bury St Edmunds fourteen months earlier. Other cases followed.

With the departure of the GIs the clubs and canteens established for them in every sizable community closed down. The American Red Cross moved out of the Bishop's Palace in Norwich in October; its Services Club had been accommodated

---

*"Operation War Brides" got into its stride before the end of January. A transit camp was created in the old army barracks at Tidworth; after assembling there, the brides and children went to Southampton, and seventeen specially converted ships, including the two Queens, took them to New York.

B17's of the USAAF 100th Bomb Group seen at Linz, Austria in May, collecting French prisoners-of-war from Austrian prison camps. *Photo courtesy of Ian Hawkins*

there for two and a half years. Often 120,000 men and women had passed through the club in a single month, with as many as one thousand staying overnight. The Athenaeum Canteen in Bury St Edmunds closed after an estimated million and a half servicemen and women had passed through[4].

Even before the European war ended a few prisoners-of-war had found their way back to Britain. Three who were released by Patton's 3rd US Army from a camp near Frankfurt on Easter Monday were home in Ely by mid-April: Staff Sergeant Edward Carney, Sergeant Glider Pilot R. W. Liles and Trooper Joseph Nightingale. They brought the first vivid accounts of the "Death Marches" which the Germans had organized when camps lay in the path of the Allied armies. All three of them had taken part in a four-hundred-mile trek across Germany from a camp at Sagan overrun by the Red Army, covering about twelve miles each day for thirty-five days. Four thousand prisoners-of-war had begun that march and only two thousand survived. Men had collapsed like flies from starvation and exhaustion as the Germans drove them forward, and there were deaths every day.

With such stories in circulation the task of getting all ex-prisoners-of-war back to Britain was approached as one of the greatest urgency. By the end of July, the initial recovery missions had been completed, but 42,000 British airmen were still unaccounted for and their fate was unknown. A Missing Research and Enquiry Service was set up to try to locate them.

By far the biggest movement of people in 1945 was the sudden migration of displaced persons of all European nations — and now this included Germans*. Vast numbers of former inmates of concentration camps, slave-labour camps and prisoner-of-war camps wandered aimlessly in a wrecked and dangerous countryside. For the plight of these poor people the Germans carried responsibility, but now the Germans themselves were sharing their affliction. In east and west — but especially where they faced and feared the advance of the Red Army — Germans abandoned their homes (where these still existed) and took to the roads. Soon there were an estimated two million of them carrying their bundles of belongings and searching for shelter. Churchill confessed in a letter to his wife:

> My heart is saddened by the tales of the masses of German women and children flying along the roads everywhere, in 40-mile long columns, to the west, before the advancing armies. I am clearly convinced that they deserve it; but that does not remove it from one's gaze. The misery of the whole world appals me.[6]

As the Allied armies closed in on the German heartland and the Nazi system disintegrated, an effort was made to clear all the camps so that none should be in use when overrun. The Death Marches of prisoners-of-war were paralleled by similar marches by those concentration camp inmates who were still alive. The only difference was that these men, women and children were treated with greater brutality[7].

Millions of Germans in their turn were expelled from the Russian-occupied zones. The Big Three leaders agreed at Potsdam in June that the frontiers of Germany should be revised, and that those of German extraction who had been living before the war in parts of Poland, Czechoslovakia and Hungary should be removed "in an orderly and humane manner".

In a Commons adjournment debate in October the Ipswich MP Mr Richard Stokes quoted reports that four and a half million were to be thus expelled, at the rate of three hundred thousand a day, including twenty thousand a day from Poland and six thousand a day from Czechoslovakia. "My appeal is that the government should do everything in its power to stop this ghastly process — first of all on humanitarian grounds", he said. "The horror it is going to bring on comparatively innocent people simply boggles the imagination." He suggested that such treatment might sow the seeds of another war, and he urged the British government to make "whatever protest they can in whatever quarter".

---

*Post-war estimates of the number of Europeans resettled, evacuated or expelled between 1944 and 1952 ranged from fourteen million to thirty million. These figures exclude six million who died in transit or as a direct result of forced migration.

The Under-Secretary of State for Foreign Affairs, Mr Hector McNeill, replied that "they are Germans and, either through their rulers or themselves, they have visited on Poles, Czechs and Russians, Christians as well as Jews, monstrous cruelties". The government, he added, had no information about the arrangements which were being put in hand; some of the figures mentioned were speculative. But he suggested that between two and a quarter and two and a half million Germans in Czechoslovakia, half a million in Hungary and perhaps more than ten million in Poland might be moved.

Stokes raised the matter again on 5th November. McNeill then said that Britain had agreed to accept one and a quarter million Germans into its occupation zone in Germany, and had made contingency plans to deal with four million. He declared that it was impossible to know how many had arrived. "The movement of these people is so irregular", he explained. "Even if it were continuous, we have not the manpower there on the spot to make accurate accounts."

On 20th November the Allied Control Commission in Berlin approved plans for six and a half million German refugees from Poland, Czechoslovakia, Austria and Hungary to be redistributed: 1,500,000 to the British zone, 2,750,000 to the Russian zone, 2,250,000 to the American zone, and 150,000 to the French zone.

Some of the East Anglian battalions in Germany found themselves busy handling problems involved in these population movements. After the capture of Bremen and the signing of the surrender, the 1st Battalion of the Royal Norfolks was based at Solingen, the 1st Battalion of the Suffolks at Enger, and the 2nd Battalion of the Essex Regiment at Unna, near Dortmund; they were all drawn into the task.

In the displaced persons camps, it was necessary to ensure that slave-labourers did not try to exact revenge. There were some attacks by Russians on Germans. In the Suffolks' area there were twenty-five incidents in June alone, though none was classed as serious. The battalion reported continual movement of prisoners-of-war and displaced persons back to their own countries, through camps which were opened for "westbound" and "eastbound". The majority were eastbound—Russians and Poles—but some were Italians moving south[8]. According to the Essex battalion records in the fifty square miles just east of the Ruhr for which they were responsible, "there was rape, murder and looting by the Russians, and counter-action by the Germans"[9], raids and shooting affrays, and at least one running battle.

Eventually things were brought under control, and an original total of ten thousand Russian displaced persons in this area was gradually reduced as they were packed into repatriation trains. Before they left some of them made up football teams and played friendly games against the Essex men.

The plight of the wandering homeless hordes was vividly illustrated in the heart of East Anglia in July when a ten-year-old Ukrainian boy was brought before the juvenile magistrates in Long Melford. Son of a prosperous merchant in

The final parade at a USAAF base before departure from the UK to the USA.

Photo courtesy of Ian Hawkins

Kharkov, he had been only six when the war overwhelmed the city. He was the only survivor of his family, and a German army unit adopted him. He waited upon a German general, travelled across the Mediterranean into North Africa and thence to Italy, and then, as the tide of war changed, the orphan passed from German into American hands.

He was "adopted" by a GI from Chicago who spoke Ukrainian, and was fitted out with a small US army uniform which bore sergeant's stripes and a purple heart. He stayed with this American's unit until VE-Day. When it was returning to the US, its ship called at a British port and the boy went with a party of GIs to London. He became separated from his companions and went to the American Red Cross Club in Piccadilly, where another American GI who could speak Ukrainian took charge of him and later took him to the USAAF base at Lavenham. The officers there handed him over to the civil authorities, and he was brought before the Long Melford court as a minor in need of care and protection. He was put in an institution at Bury St Edmunds pending a further hearing, but absconded to the US base at Honington. The magistrates then agreed that he should stay there pending completion of procedures for him to be adopted by the family of an American soldier. Just as these arrangements were being completed, he disappeared again. As the year ended a search for him was continuing in London.

In Germany the slave-workers who had been liberated and repatriated had to be replaced on German farms, and the Allied Military Government was anxious to get suitable German soldiers back to work. Fourteen centres were set up in north Germany, where most of the German uniformed services were herded in concentration areas during the course of May. At one of these in Schleswig-Holstein, just north of the Kiel Canal, officers and men of the 65th Anti-Tank

Regiment RA (Norfolk Yeomanry) acted as a "demobilization detachment" to the German army. They dealt with 75,000 men during June, including the provision of armed escorts to get them to the farms.

German prisoners-of-war were also brought to Britain to work in agriculture, replacing Italian prisoners-of-war who now began to return home. There were still 118,000 Italians here in August 1945, categorized as "co-operators"; and most of them were engaged in farm work. They began to be repatriated after the harvest. Some farmers had expressed great dissatisfaction with them and were glad to see them depart; many others found them good workers. Perhaps the contrasting attitudes were accounted for in the final sentence of this note by a Bury St Edmunds woman on the experience of a farming friend:

> Mary's husband is fighting in Italy, as a major. He told Win to treat the Italian prisoner-of-war farm assistants well, as the Italians treated him well. Win said they seemed scared at first, but Stan had found them excellent workers, and they were nice fellows. One said in two years it was the first farm where he had been treated like a human being . . . [10]

An *East Anglian Daily Times* columnist, "Lavengro", wrote of the Italians: "Everywhere there are complaints about their indolence . . . Cannot some steps be taken to make them earn their keep?" Newmarket Urban District Council protested to the War Office about the freedom they were permitted. A soldier on leave wrote to the *Eastern Daily Press* to complain:

> While we were at home for a short time after fighting in Africa and Sicily we saw in some cases Italian prisoners in better billets than ourselves, and being granted unbelievable privileges. As a nation we are too good-hearted . . .

The Ministry of Agriculture policy was that every Italian withdrawn from the farms to be repatriated would be replaced by a German prisoner-of-war. There were nearly two hundred thousand such Germans in Great Britain when the war ended, and at first some were used to clear mines from beaches and cliff-tops. By August their number had almost doubled, and more than half were working on farms or in forestry. Some others were engaged in housing site preparation, road-making and civil engineering. Many of them were housed in the fifty prisoner-of-war camps situated in East Anglia, a number of which were former American air bases, but when winter came there were still some living in tents. They wore green or brown battle-dress with a large circle or diamond in a contrasting colour on tunic or trousers. There was a strict no-fraternization policy.

A small number of the Germans who were brought to Britain were soon sent home again. They were screened, and if they were judged to be trustworthy and liberal minded—and if they had special skills the Allied Control Commission could use in rebuilding a new Germany—they were released. By the end of the year over five hundred miners, bank officials, lawyers, factory managers and police[11] had been sent back. Some sick and wounded were also allowed to leave.

A sombre mood settled on those who remained in the German prisoner-of-war camps. The British Cabinet had resolved back in September 1944 that they should undergo a programme of re-education, using lectures, publications, visual aids and English teaching; but this scheme suffered from an acute shortage of German speakers[12]. There was no difficulty, however, in decreeing that a twenty-minute horror film depicting the liberation of the Belsen concentration camp must be seen by all the prisoners, including the sick and wounded. Some of the men found their own diversions, one of which was the carving of 'treenware' from odd scraps of wood — birds and animals, platters, rocking horses and religious images.

An official Red Cross representative who visited camps for the first time in August told the prisoners-of-war that he could give them no hope of early repatriation. The Red Cross calculated that they would be looking after prisoners-of-war for the next two years. This news had a sledgehammer effect. The prisoners were well aware of the chaos that had overwhelmed their country: that masses of the ten million Germans evacuated from bombed cities were roaming aimlessly in the countryside, and that three million foreign workers were still in Germany. They felt intense anxiety about family and friends with whom they had lost touch[13], and about whom they could obtain no news because postal services had almost completely ceased*.

In September the British authorities made a first effort to put prisoners-of-war in touch with their dispersed families, inviting them to send postcards bearing the printed words: "A member of the defeated Wehrmacht seeks his next of kin." By November prisoners were allowed to send one postcard every week[14], and by the end of the year postal services to the US and British zones were beginning to flow, slowly and irregularly.

Perhaps it was natural that very few, apart from the International Red Cross, took much interest in the German prisoners. One who did was the Ipswich MP, Richard Stokes. When the Minister of Works told the Commons in November that he had 27,700 Germans at his disposal, Stokes fired a series of questions. Were they being paid "a full and proper wage" or were they being "used as slaves"? When would they be sent home?†

---

*There was no postal service to Berlin or the Soviet zone of Germany until February 1946.

†For the majority of them, it turned out to be in two and a half years time. Herbert Morrison told the Commons in February 1946: "The great majority of these prisoners are engaged in work of the highest importance for which suitable British labour is not available. No arrangements have been made or are at present in contemplation for the repatriation of the German prisoners. On the contrary, arrangements are in hand to bring further German prisoners to this country from other areas in considerable numbers, to make good the loss of Italians and to supplement the prisoner of war labour force." In March 1946 100,800 Germans were employed in British agriculture; 4,800 were in timber production, the fertilizer industry, tyre production and so on; 30,000 were working on housing sites or in the construction industry; and 2,000 were employed on railways and roads, in quarries, or on canals. The highest number of German prisoners-of-war in Britain was 402,200, in September 1946[15]. Repatriation then began and was completed in May 1948. Some who did not want to return to Russian-occupied territory opted to stay in Britain or to go to Canada, Australia or New Zealand.

CHAPTER EIGHT

Out Of The Chrysalis

A FTER YEARS tightly constrained by compulsions, restrictions and shortages, the people were palpitating to break out and spread their wings in a brave new world. In the early weeks of 1945 they began to shed some layers of the chrysalis of regulations that had governed their lives.

The first thing to go, during January, was the fireguard roster. Every factory, every office block and every residential street had had its fire-watching parties on duty every night for more than four years, each armed with stirrup pumps and buckets of sand, ready to deal with incendiary bombs. These duties, compulsory for all civilians, had been relaxed in most places four months earlier; street parties had been stood down and the numbers of firewatchers required at business premises reduced. The fireguard was now disbanded—except in Great Yarmouth, Ipswich and a few other towns near the coast, where it was maintained a few weeks longer. In May five hundred men and women who had served part-time in the National Fire Service in Cambridgeshire, Huntingdonshire, Newmarket and the Isle of Ely gathered for a stand-down parade in Cambridge.

Balloon Command was wound up during February, and the bulbous grey barrage balloons and their trailing cables disappeared from the skies. The air raid warning system was discontinued from midday on 2nd May and the wailing sirens were heard no more. The "dim-out" ended for most people on 23rd April and it was no longer an offence to show lights from buildings, but these restrictions remained in a five-mile-deep belt around the coast until 10th May.

Not until 15th July was full street lighting permitted again. This delay was the consequence of fuel shortage, which soon led to reimposition of restrictions. Cambridge and Norwich resumed full street lighting in July, but from 27th August switched everything off at midnight in response to a Ministry of Fuel appeal.

The Royal Observer Corps finally closed in May. Special constables continued their duties until 15th June. By early summer there were stand-down parades throughout the region almost every week, such as the special farewell parade of the Cambridge Borough Special Constabulary, Civil Defence and Fire Guard on Parker's Piece in July. In Norwich the employment of all full-time ARP officers and staff was terminated by the end of August. The ARP department was completely closed down a month later, all its equipment collected and either stored or disposed of. In Cambridge stirrup pumps were sold for 7s 6d each. By September most of the Civil Defence and non-combatant organizations throughout the eastern region had been disbanded.

Girls of the Royal Observer Corps 18 Group, on stand-down parade at Birch aerodrome in July, are inspected by Air Commodore Finlay Crerar, Commandant of the R.O.C.

Photo courtesy of Mrs Hervey Benham

The war left behind a massive litter of defensive works: steel scaffolding and barbed wire, minefields, concrete pill-boxes, road blocks, public shelters, static water tanks and temporary buildings of all kinds. It was clear that some of the concrete would take years to remove, but a start had to be made somewhere. The services gave a lead. In January the navy blew up with explosives road blocks on Bolland Quay at Great Yarmouth, and removed many of their training huts. The military began to clear the east-coast beaches and by early March had dealt with extensive stretches of the foreshore at Lowestoft, Southwold, Walberswick, Felixstowe and Aldeburgh. Much wire and tubular scaffold remained, however, to delineate the limits of clearance. This work went on all year; it was dangerous and there were casualties. Two teenage youths were killed by a mine in March while rabbiting near the coast at East Mersea, within a mile of their homes. Later two Royal Engineers sappers were killed while seeking four missing mines on the North Denes at Lowestoft.

The "missing" mines were a problem. A careful record had been made when they were laid, and the objective was to account for them all one by one. But stormy weather had disturbed some of them, some had been accidentally detonated by stray animals and others had been washed in from the sea. Wherever an area appeared to have been disturbed since the mines were laid, it was carefully swept by detectors and all accumulations of shingle and sand were thoroughly explored to the apparent depth of the disturbance. If all mines could not be accounted for in actual mines or craters, then the army, after clearance, would only issue a qualified safety certificate. In many resorts this left the local authorities feeling distinctly uneasy about permitting public access.

Local authorities meanwhile gave priority to sealing off the entrances to underground shelters at schools, and this was done during their summer holidays. In September tenders were invited for demolition of surface street shelters.

The rehabilitation of the seaside resorts began slowly. At Whitsun nearly all the hotels and boarding-houses in Lowestoft remained either requisitioned or empty, and there was little or no accommodation for visitors. When the year ended the Admiralty still held thirteen hotels and boarding-houses, eighteen business premises and twenty-five private residences. Fourteen hotels and boarding-houses requisitioned by the War Office in Sheringham were not released until the end of November, and hotels and boarding-houses in Cromer remained under requisition until some weeks later.

By early summer the government-sponsored British Restaurants which had made available cheap meals for war workers were being closed everywhere. Private restaurants and cafes were reopening. Not everyone was pleased. The *Cambridge Daily News* published a reader's letter complaining that the new restaurants were full of eclairs, fancy chocolate cakes and cream buns, while in ordinary shops there was an "apparent lack of food in this town . . . the shortage is worse than ever".

As the summer weather settled in rumours circulated that petrol rationing was about to end, and motorists rushed to prepare themselves. In Norwich five hundred cars which had been laid up during the war were relicensed and nearly a thousand driving licences were issued during the second half of May. Hopes were dashed, however, by a Ministry of Fuel announcement that ration books were being printed for another six-month period, beginning on 1st September.

There was further disappointment when the Ministry, having announced on 16th August a twenty-five per cent increase in the basic petrol ration to allow 150 miles' motoring a month—with probable further relaxations later—cancelled the concession within a week or so because American Lend-Lease supplies had been cut off. There was a slight compensation: the price of motor spirit was reduced by twopence to 1s 11½d per gallon.

Petrol coupons rose in value on the black market. Towards the end of the year two Cambridge men were sent for trial charged with being concerned in the theft of coupons for thirty-nine thousand gallons of petrol from the Eastern Regional Petroleum Office.

Many motorists were so out of practice that they needed to learn again how to drive; while they were doing so a procession of drivers came before the magistrates for a variety of offences, the most common being failure to stop at a "halt" sign.

Advertisements began to appear in July announcing that new vehicles would soon be on sale. A Norwich Motor Company advertisement in the *Eastern Daily Press* read: "Early delivery of new Hillman-Minx saloons can now be obtained, subject to Ministry of War Transport licence. Price £310 ex-works, plus Purchase Tax."

Many consumer products were returning to the shops in small quantities. Another July advertisement read:

> We are receiving at regular intervals small stocks of wash boilers, boiling rings, kettles, irons, electric fires, table lamps, ceiling fittings and shades. In addition, we shall be able to supply in the near future a small number of cookers, washing machines, water softeners, refrigerators and vacuum cleaners. Intending purchasers should call at our showrooms and have their name entered on the priority list. They will then be notified by letter as supplies become available.

Other advertisements provided a monthly catalogue of new 78 rpm gramophone records. These were mainly classical items but they included Victor Silvester and his Ballroom Orchestra playing "Pablo the Dreamer", Lou Preager and his Orchestra playing "The Hokey Cokey" and Frank Sinatra singing "Embraceable You".

British Railways announced many additional trains and promised that the winter service starting on 1st October would bring a speed-up of main-line services.

The east-coast ports slowly switched back to peacetime operation but still had important duties to fulfil for the services. Harwich was one of the principal Trinity House bases, responsible for laying and maintaining hundreds of buoys needed to mark safe channels—there were nearly 350 buoys, the majority of them "lights", in the Harwich area alone. With the occupation of Germany a buoyed passage right across the North Sea to Hamburg was called for, and this task was carried out by Trinity House vessels from Harwich and Great Yarmouth.

The Royal Navy began to prepare from January for its departure from Great Yarmouth, and once Germany had been defeated things moved rapidly. The admiral's flag was hauled down at the naval barracks at sunset on 31st July, marking the closure of the base. At Sparrow's Nest the seats went back into the concert hall and the first seaside show returned.

Parkeston Quay was the headquarters of the Dutch Naval Command—Queen Wilhelmina of the Netherlands paid a visit early in 1945—and after the liberation of the country many barges laden with food, hospital equipment and clothing left Parkeston and Harwich for Rotterdam. In September Parkeston quays were still fully occupied by navy vessels and boats of the British Army on the Rhine, and no date was available for resumption of the normal service to the Hook of Holland.

HMS *Beehive* at Felixstowe, with its headquarters at the Pier Hotel, did not close until 18th October—the last Light Coastal Force base on the east coast. It had

LNER
MORE
TRAINS

From 1st October the LNER is running a number of additional and faster trains.   These include

WEEKDAYS

NORWICH THORPE

Dep. 11.50 a.m.	Ipswich - -	- arr. 12.48 p.m.
RESTAURANT CAR	Liverpool St.	- arr. 2.30 p.m.
Dep. 2.20 p.m.	Ely - - -	- arr. 3.48 p.m.
	Cambridge -	- arr. 4.11 p.m.
	Liverpool St.	- arr. 6.4 p.m.

IPSWICH

Dep. 5.35 p.m.   Norwich Thorpe arr. 7.20 p.m.

LIVERPOOL STREET

Dep. 12.30 p.m.   Norwich Thorpe arr. 3.13 p.m.
Dep. 6.40 p.m.   Norwich Thorpe arr. 9.20 p.m.
RESTAURANT CAR

Lowestoft dep. 10 a.m., Yarmouth 10.15, Norwich 11.10 to York, arriving 4.46 p.m.

York dep. 10.35 a.m. to Norwich arriving 5.2 p.m. Yarmouth 6.7, Lowestoft 6.3 p.m.

The improvements represent the most that can be done but the LNER is very glad to make them available

LONDON AND NORTH EASTERN RAILWAY

been operational since June 1940 and its motor torpedo boats and gunboats had carried out more than four thousand anti-E-boat patrols during their efforts to protect North Sea convoys. In the period just before VE-Day seventy light coastal craft were operating there, with a complement of about 2,500 officers, ratings and WRNS.

At the time of VE-Day the navy had 1,533 vessels engaged in the enormous task of sweeping up mines in British coastal waters. By mid-July an area two miles out to sea, from the river Nene to the river Minsmere, had been cleared for shipping. At the beginning of September the *Eastern Daily Press* wrote of "drifters jostling on the heels of the minesweepers". Nearly all fishermen had left the Navy and drifters and trawlers were being handed back "as rapidly as circumstances permit".

Agriculture, the other source of food supplies, was experiencing difficulties. Farmers declared they were at their wits' end during the harvest season because of labour difficulties. They declared they were seriously behind with cutting and carting their cereal crops, and that much that had been stacked had not been thatched. Some German prisoners-of-war were being allocated to them, usually as replacements for departing Italians, but that only gave them a new subject of complaint: that the three pounds a week they were required to pay the Ministry for each of these men was excessive. Not until December did the government offer some hope that agricultural workers and some rural craftsmen—blacksmiths, wheelwrights and saddlers—would soon be released from the forces.

The girls of the Women's Land Army were also unhappy; they were to be denied equal treatment with other conscripts when they were released. They demanded wartime gratuities on the same scale as those to be given to Civil Defence workers, and also adequate clothing and coupon allowances, and full maintenance during free government training for other jobs. In south Essex nearly a hundred girls went on strike, and forty WLA girls at the Ipswich hostel staged a one-day stoppage in sympathy. The strike was settled after a few days but it had repercussions. Land Girls from Cambridge and district, acting on their own initiative but with the backing of the National Union of Agricultural Workers, held a protest meeting in the Central Labour Hall in Cambridge and elected a provisional committee of eight to organize a campaign.

New life was flowing back strongly into the inland towns. A returning serviceman reported his impressions in a letter to the editor of the *Eastern Daily Press* published during June:

> Norwich seems to me to be recovering her old vitality and the busy atmosphere of her shopping centres very quickly. I hear far fewer grumbles about rationing and the difficulties of shopping than two years ago . . . Train services from London and bus facilities in the city are quite good, considering all difficulties; officials in the city offices and banks lack nothing in courtesy and helpfulness . . . It is good to be home in the clean pleasant Norwich streets . .

Those American servicemen who were still in East Anglia were relaxed and happy. One of them afterwards recalled his visit to Cambridge at this time:

> The river was crowded with American soldiers who were snarling up traffic in a hopeless way, but the air was so full of good humour and high spirits that no one seemed to mind the imminent danger of capsizing. Drifting lazily downstream we heard the bells of St Mary's ringing the changes, while we saw the buildings at their most beautiful. Writing now in nostalgia in the Arkansas winter, it seems to me that I reached the very summit of human happiness during those sun-lit hours on the Cam.[1]

Press censorship in Great Britain—which theoretically had been voluntary during the war—was formally wound up on 2nd September, exactly six years after it had been introduced. Virtually all the restrictions had in practice been disregarded since VE-Day, but newspapers continued to suffer another kind of restraint, a serious limitation on the supply of paper. Even as 1945 ended the

Eastern Daily Press, for example, had newsprint supplies only sufficient for four-page issues, except for one six-pager on Saturdays.

The newspaper was generous, however, in its tribute to those who had had to safeguard security in the region and in particular to the Regional Commissioner, Sir Will Spens. In a leading article it wrote:

> In the wrong hands and exercised in the gauleiter spirit, they might very easily have made endless trouble and difficulty throughout the area. Sir Will Spens has not only known what to do but—what in some ways has been even more important—what to avoid. He has kept his office clear of any suggestion of truculence or dictatorship, such as might so readily have found expression in the exercise of such extensive powers, and he has made everyone feel that the regional office was there to be helpful.

For the great majority of people the touchstone of normality was demobilization. How quickly could men get back to their homes and their jobs? This concerned not only families but also the factories. There was keen interest in the return of manpower and womenpower to industry and commerce.

In March, before the war in Europe ended, the War Minister in Churchill's coalition government, Sir James Grigg, announced that a great many of those with the longest service would be released from the forces after the defeat of Germany, and that the maximum tour of unrelieved overseas service would then be cut to three years. The government also announced that as men and women were released they would receive a tax-free gratuity—ten shillings for each complete month of service for those in the ranks and twenty-five shillings for the lowest officer ranks.

A less welcome announcement was that there would be a new call-up, including a substantial number of men who had hitherto been in reserved occupations. Mr Ernest Bevin explained in May that the government's plan was for a "comprehensive plan for reallocation of manpower, and not for demobilisation". Release from the forces would begin on 18th June, and it was estimated that 750,000 would be out by the end of the year, most of them from the Army. The call-up of men up to the age of thirty would continue, and he warned that there was likely to be some form of national service for a number of years. Mr Bevin added that conscription of women would end immediately. Women with household responsibilities would no longer be required to take jobs. If they were already employed they would be free to leave, but he urged those who could to continue in employment.

Concurrently with these announcements the Board of Trade set up special regional organizations to assist industry in the transition to peacetime production. An Eastern Regional Controller established his headquarters in Cambridge. Leading manufacturers and industrialists were invited to conferences in Cambridge and Norwich to hear the government's interim plans for conversion from war to peace, for reallocation of manpower and for relaxation of controls on premises. They were told by government officials that until the defeat of Japan fifty per cent of war production would continue, as would controls. A

Resettlement Advice Office was opened in Cambridge.

Eastern counties businessmen put their heads together to launch self-help schemes. In Ipswich a Private Traders' Association was formed in March, aiming to put emphasis on "personal service". Cromer set up a Chamber of Trade and Commerce, asserting that "the next few years will be critical in rebuilding Cromer as a tourist centre". These examples were followed elsewhere.

The first releases from the forces were of women and men of forty-eight and over, and came on schedule. Some passed through the Royal Naval Patrol Service dispersal centre at Lowestoft on 17th June. Others among the first to be demobbed were a limited number with special skills or qualifications needed for the repair of bomb damage in some of the most badly stricken towns and cities, which included Great Yarmouth and Lowestoft.

With a change of government after the general election, the whole subject of demobilization was re-examined. But when Prime Minister Attlee broadcast on the anniversary of the outbreak of war, 3rd September, he insisted that the demobilization programme must stand. "I would solemnly warn the nation that the result of breaking away from a carefully planned scheme is chaos", he said. "This happened at the end of the last war." The civilian labour force would have to be increased by five millions if all men and women were to be placed in jobs as they came out of the forces, he explained.

The Cabinet conferred with the service chiefs again in October, however, and decided that some acceleration of demobilization was possible: it was announced that one and a half million men and women would be demobbed by the end of 1945 and three million by June 1946.

Apart from the men and women released from the forces, alternative work had to be found for those no longer required in the munitions industry. There were still three million thus employed in October, but the Minister of Labour, Mr George Isaacs, declared that numbers would be steadily reduced.

East Anglia contained only a small proportion of the factories which had turned out the weapons of war, but even so redeployment of the labour force involved was no small problem. Factories in Norfolk, Suffolk, Essex, Hertfordshire, Bedfordshire, Cambridgeshire, Huntingdonshire and the Isle of Ely had employed 130,000 on aircraft production and sixteen thousand on manufacture of radio, radar and electrical equipment. They had built over ten thousand aircraft of different types for the RAF, including over seven hundred Halifaxes for Bomber Command.

The nature of some of the problems was illustrated in September when a Norwich factory which had employed five hundred women on production of batteries was closed down. Efforts were made to redeploy them. The *Eastern Daily Press* reported: "The vast majority have expressed a desire, in preliminary interviews at the factory, to remain in factory work, where the comradeship and social life of the war years made considerable appeal . . .". Norwich Labour

Exchange had 650 vacancies at the time, but only about 250 of them were in factories. Some of the displaced workers were placed in the footwear and clothing industry, but these factories were unable to expand their production because of the rationing of scarce raw materials.

In some areas there were acute labour shortages. Hotels and hospitals were seriously short of staff. The schools needed seventy thousand more teachers. The government invited would-be recruits to the teaching profession to submit their names, and a thousand immediately did so. Mr R. A. Butler, Minister of Education, announced that three new training colleges would be opened forthwith, two for women and one for men, and he promised that more would be opened as more applications were received.

Many workers in civilian employment remained subject to strict control and could not change jobs without Ministry of Labour approval. A Cambridge milk roundsman who left his job without permission was among many who came before the courts and were fined.

The struggle back to normality was not only taking place in England; it was

TELEVISION

Our pre-war reputation for Television Service is precious to us, and we assure all potential receivers that we shall endeavour to keep and enhance this reputation when Television programmes recommence.

Miller's STUDIO
SIDNEY STREET, CAMBRIDGE

Anticipating the return of a television service, Millers of Cambridge placed this advertisement. *Cambridge Daily News* an almost universal problem. The men of several East Anglian battalions of the army were deeply engaged in it on the Continent. As we have seen earlier, they had settled to occupation duties after the German surrender. Apart from their responsibilities in connection with displaced persons, the Army of Occupation had diverse duties: battlefield clearance and disposal of enemy war materials and installations, patrols and house searches, security of army lines of communication, road and rail bridges, locks and sluice gates, ammunition dumps and food stores, factories and warehouses, and assistance to the Allied Military Government concerned with camps and prisons.

The Suffolks reported "the most negligible sabotage—not always attributable to Germans. The enemy showed themselves only too anxious to obey all orders."[2] The 2nd Battalion of the Essex Regiment set up the first unit educational establishment in the British Army of Occupation, known as "Essex College"; it served over 250 students before they returned to civilian life. This battalion left Unna in November 1945 and moved to Berlin.

Meanwhile the 5th Battalion of the Essex Regiment, which had taken part in the race to Lubeck, established headquarters at Krumesse and launched "Operation Eclipse": the rounding up and disarming of prisoners, segregation of SS men and other dangerous types, collection of small arms into dumps for destruction, and the assembly of guns and armed vehicles in parks. Krumesse was on the inter-zonal border and liaison visits were exchanged with the Red Army. In October the battalion moved to Bleckede on the Elbe and was given the task of internal security in the Kreis Luneburg, which included guarding former staff of the Belsen concentration camp until they were brought to trial at Luneburg a few weeks later.

Amid these occupation duties there was still time for flag marches, for beating the retreat and for ceremonial guard-mounting parades—all of which, it was confidently believed, greatly impressed the local populations.

The Dutch town of Weert celebrated its progress towards peacetime normality with a big event on 22nd September, the anniversary of its liberation. The 1st Battalion of the Suffolks, which had played so important a role, was invited to return and join in. Two officers and forty men, with the padre, went. Every house was flagged and there were orange streamers everywhere. After a service in the big medieval church in the market square everyone went to the Town Hall, where the Burgomaster read a speech in English asking the battalion to accept a scroll and silver shield as a mark of esteem[3].

The 3rd Division left Europe early in October for duty in Egypt and Palestine, completing the journey in three stages: a two-day rail journey in Toulon crowded into old German coaches; then a voyage to Alexandria in a converted French pleasure cruiser, the *Ville d'Oran*, carrying four times its peacetime complement; and finally another rail journey, this time in freight wagons, to a tented camp in the desert at Tahag near the Suez Canal. By that time about half the men of the Suffolk battalion had been demobilized and had been replaced by reinforcements of three hundred men, most of them brought from East Anglia.

For the 1st Essex, in India, there was much training during 1945, but no specific task assigned; a brief expectation that it would form part of the occupation force in Japan was quickly disappointed. At Uruli camp, seventeen miles from Poona, there was a brief lift to spirits when the battalion linked up with a large draft from the UK, mostly men of AA units of East Anglian origin. As 1945 ended the 1st Essex seemed settled in India, ready to help with the emerging problems of the last days of the British Raj.

Another Essex battalion, the 1/4th, was helping to restore peace in Greece. It had arrived there late in 1944 from Italy, where it had suffered grievously in the bitter campaign to capture Monte Cassino. It was then given an almost equally unpleasant task: winkling out guerrilla fighters of the "People's National Army of Liberation" (ELAS) who, after fighting the German occupation troops, had occupied Athens. The British authorities regarded them as communists and when they refused to disarm (because, they said, right-wing elements were not being disbanded) British tanks went into action. Hundreds of Greeks were killed or wounded before ELAS resistance virtually ceased in Athens on 5th January 1945 and their units withdrew to the hills. A truce was signed a week later.

This struggle provoked strong reaction in the United Kingdom. Churchill told the Commons that the communists planned to seize power once the British withdrew. But the anti-coalition candidate who won the Chelmsford by-election soon afterwards made much of his opposition to British policy in Greece.

After the fighting in the Greek capital the Essex battalion moved to Edhessa, the capital of western Macedonia. It was made responsible for two thousand square miles, which included the whole of the Greek–Yugoslav frontier and part of the frontier with Albania. Roads, transportation and municipal services were in chaos and the area was a happy hunting ground for bandits, but gradually the battalion restored order and progressively passed over control to the Greeks. So successfully did they establish good relations that in September the municipal council of Edhessa designated the battalion its "honorary regiment" and conferred the Freedom of the city on its commanding officer, Lieutenant Colonel A. Lovelace. On the day of this ceremony the heavens opened and the streets were flooded. Colonel Lovelace afterwards related:

> In an endeavour to clear the water in front of the Town Hall, someone had taken out the manhole cover from a drain. Flushed with congratulations and Greek wine, I left the Hall, saluting obvious personages, went towards the staff car and disappeared down the drain.

His adjutant added this postscript" "The C.O. was so keen in his new-found civic responsibilities that he started a tour of inspection of the city's sewers right away."[4]

CHAPTER NINE

Laying New Foundations

MANY COMMUNITIES began to plan their post-war reconstruction and development long before the war ended. Though aspirations were high it was everywhere appreciated that an immense task confronted them. German bombs had destroyed enormous numbers of houses, shops, factories and public buildings—in some places on such a scale that major exercises in town replanning were appropriate. Apart from this restoration there was a widely perceived need to upgrade the structures of community life. Mr J. F. Wright, Norfolk County Secretary of the National Farmers' Union, wrote in the *Eastern Daily Press:*

> We hope that the coming year will see foundations laid for the improvement of conditions in the countryside: more and better cottages, smaller and up-to-date farmhouses with modern farm buildings and equipment, a vast extension of electricity and water supplies. Such amenities will attract more people to rural life and give greater encouragement to those who have faced the difficulties of the past.

Some sought to damp down what they considered excessive expectations. The Deputy Regional Commissioner, the Earl of Cranbrook, told a conference in Bury St Edmunds which discussed "Village Life after the War" that he did not think a universal water and drainage grid was practical within the next generation, and he advised them to concentrate on getting an electricity supply to the rural areas. Discussing the housing situation, he admitted that he had been horrified and shocked at the conditions in which a large number of people had to exist: "in many of these houses I would not be allowed to put my cows and sell clean milk".

Beyond question, housing presented the most important and urgent post-war problem. No new houses had been built for six years and in addition many houses had been completely destroyed by bombs. Those who had married during these years were now impatient to set up home and start families—if they could get a roof over their heads.

The first task was to deal with the houses that had been damaged but could be repaired. In the eastern counties 202,328 properties were in this category, according to War Damage Commission official figures. In Lowestoft, one of the most severely battered East Anglian towns, there were 9,433 war-damaged houses. A labour force of 528 was assembled to repair them; some were workers in the industry who were directed to the town from other parts of the country by the Ministry of Labour, and two hundred—more than a third—were German prisoners-of-war. These latter were accommodated in tents while they prepared a site in North Lowestoft, and they were paid not in cash but in tokens exchangeable in a camp canteen. The rate was three farthings an hour, increased to three halfpence an hour if their work was pronounced satisfactory. Thus after forty-eight hours' labour they had the equivalent of six shillings to spend. By mid-December eighty-five per cent of the damaged houses had been restored.

A considerable number of privately owned houses was standing empty. Rents were controlled at pre-war levels while, in conditions of great shortage, house prices had risen sharply. So private owners sold their houses rather than offering them for rental. A reader of the *Cambridge Daily News* complained in a letter to the editor that three thousand pounds were being asked for three-bedroom houses for which the price had been nine hundred pounds before the war. He called the sellers "sharks".

In Great Yarmouth over 990 houses stood empty until, soon after the election of the new Labour government, the Ministry of Health conferred powers on local authorities to requisition any such properties. A 1939 defence regulation was used to secure rapid action; it decreed that "as soon as a notice has been posted on premises the property is requisitioned from that date". Many councils in the region made use of this power during the second half of 1945. Ipswich, and Great Yarmouth among them.

The overwhelming majority of people needed houses to rent; comparatively few aspired to home ownership. That houses for rental were almost impossible to find was graphically illustrated by this letter published in the *Cambridge Daily News:*

> My wife has been trying for some time past to find unfurnished accommodation, but her efforts have been fruitless. I am now at home on leave from the Army and am informed by the owner of the house I am at present in that my wife and myself will have to be out of the rooms by October, otherwise an ejection order will be applied for. Already five days of my leave have passed, and after answering adverts, advertising myself in local papers, calling at various government offices, etc. and knocking from door to door, almost begging for accommodation, I am still unable to find anything. Isn't there, in the whole of Cambridge, some person who would be willing to offer my wife accommodation in an extreme emergency, especially those in large houses?

Everyone recognized the scale of need. The coalition government published a White Paper on housing in March assessing the national need at 1,250,000 new houses. It promised that the first two post-war years would be treated as a period of national emergency.

In Norwich the waiting list for council houses to rent contained 4,500 names, in Ipswich 1,500, in Chelmsford 1,500 and in Colchester 1,100. In Cambridge in June there was a waiting list of 2,335, and about seventy-five new applications were being received every week. Well over half the families on the list had no separate accommodation of their own, and of these 695 were servicemen's families. In addition 443 servicemen's families were living in buildings which had been condemned seven years earlier as unfit for occupation. Other people were clamouring for a chance to move into these condemned houses.

Every local authority produced estimates of the number of new dwellings it required and prepared building programmes. They set targets for the first post-war year and made provisional estimates for the following year, and they all wanted permanent houses of the traditional type. Building materials, however, were in very short supply, and the construction industry needed to be expanded and reorganized. On the other hand there were many "metal-bashing" factories no longer required for armaments which could be rapidly switched to production of components that could be assembled into temporary structures. These small houses, intended as a ten-year stop-gap solution, became known as "prefabs". The government did its best to recommend them to the public and made allocations to each local authority, but at first they were not well received. The *East Anglian Daily News* commented: "A very few years ago no one could have believed that we should have been reduced to . . . this form of makeshift accommodation." Thingoe Rural District Council resolved to decline the Ministry offer of temporary houses, declaring they would prefer to use Nissen huts vacated by the army.

There were severe restrictions on the size and design of traditional houses, presaged by a report early in the year from a committee of the Royal Institute of British Architects. This accurately forecast that the first permanent houses would lack baths, but might have small rooms into which baths could be installed later when the supply shortage had been overcome. Many such houses were built in the East Anglian countryside. The Minister of Reconstruction, Lord Woolton, told the Commons in January that the government's aim was to build three hundred thousand permanent houses in the first two years after the war ended, and to supply

A special booklet designed to be of real help to all ranks in the Services

THAT HOUSE IN CIVVY STREET

How to set about YOUR post-war housing problem
Post free — Threepence — from the
SERVICES INFORMATION BUREAU
ABBEY NATIONAL BUILDING SOCIETY
Abbey House, Baker Street, London, N.W.1

As the year began the thoughts of many were turning to the problems of finding new homes when the war ended. The Abbey National Building Society placed this advertisement in January: "That House on Civvy Street".
Cambridge Daily Press

as many temporary houses as the factories could turn out. The labour force— which at that time numbered 350,000—would be built up to eight hundred thousand in the first post-war year by release of skilled men from the forces and by training new recruits.

The councils calculated their needs and planned how best they thought they might meet them. Norwich estimated that five thousand new homes would be needed to replace those destroyed by bombs. The chairman of the Cambridge Housing Committee, Dr Alex Wood, said the town needed four thousand to five thousand new houses. Ipswich Town Council drafted a ten-year building programme for six thousand houses and expected that private enterprise would build five thousand in the same period, though it conceded that because of labour shortages the rate of building might be slower in the early years; this would have to be made up later.

Whitehall only wanted to hear about short-term objectives, however, and so the programmes submitted for approval covered only the first and second post-war years. Whitehall had to give its approval to loans required to finance the purchase of sites and the erection of houses, and Whitehall controlled the supply of labour and materials for the construction industry.

The local authorities' programmes were returned with their targets slashed. Cambridge Town Council asked for 360 new permanent houses on a site at Trumpington; and the Ministry of Health authorized only thirty-six, offering additionally three hundred temporary houses. Smaller authorities fared no better. For example, Walsingham Rural District Council put its total need at 474 houses, applied for 250 "prefabs', and was allocated forty.

Houses allocated were usually slow in materializing, and many local authorities became impatient and placed the blame squarely on Whitehall. By the summer Norwich had been promised one thousand temporary houses, but only 229 were in course of erection and a mere 128 had been completed. Tenants moved into the first eight early in September, by which time foundations were being laid for eighty-three more. At Wymondham the local MP, Mr Edwin Gooch, laid a brick of the first permanent house in mid-September, and this was the first such ceremony in the county. Most local authorities allocated their homes on a points system loaded in favour of ex-servicemen.

Great Yarmouth Town Council complained loudly about government slowness in supplying "prefabs" and authorizing priority repair of bomb-damaged houses. They were still awaiting their temporary homes two months after they had informed the ministry that they had eighty-nine sites ready. In Cambridge the first temporary houses were not ready for occupation until the end of October.

While the Churchill administration was still in office the chairman of the Cambridge Housing Committee, Dr Alex Wood, accused it of muddle, and warned: "Unless the government tackles this housing problem in an entirely different way from the way they have tackled it so far there is a good chance of a revolution in this country within the next year or two." Later he led a deputation to Whitehall, after which he declared, in June: "Both locally and nationally we are moving into an emergency of the first magnitude."

As the year ended blame was being passed back and forth between Whitehall and the counties, with widespread complaints about delays in getting authorization to proceed, or in obtaining tenders, or in actually starting work.

The shortage of building materials was a major factor in the delays. Its seriousness was shown by the restrictions placed on house-owners wanting work done on their property—they could obtain licences for only twenty-two-pounds' worth of work during the six months from 1st August to 31st January 1946. There was no restriction, however, on work they chose to do themselves.

Towards the end of the year the one- and two-year programmes were replaced by more ambitious long-term building projects. Norwich City Council, for example, approved plans for its first post-war permanent housing estate. It was to be built on 190 acres of land overlooking Old Earlham and a picturesque bend of the Yare, which it had purchased earlier in the year for thirty thousand pounds. The Norwich City Architect, Mr L. H. Hannaford, produced a plan for a new community of 1,100 permanent houses, a senior school with playing fields, nursery and infants' schools, a branch library, a community centre, a shopping centre, a church, open spaces, old people's homes and a site for a public house. This Earlham West Estate scheme was approved by the council in December and at the same time estimates were accepted for the first three hundred houses.

There was another big reconstruction task linked to housing development which confronted practically ever local authority in East Anglia: the provision of piped water supplies and sewerage disposal schemes. Most rural communities lacked these amenities, and their inhabitants had had enough of wells that dried up and privies at the end of garden paths.

When the war ended there were 377 parishes in Norfolk without a piped water supply, and there were five boroughs or urban districts where the supply was recognized to be inadequate according to a reply given by the Minister of Health, Mr Aneurin Bevan, to the MP for South-West Norfolk, Mr Sydney Dye, in the Commons on 29th November. Of about 50,500 rural dwellings in the county only 13,300 had a piped supply from public sources.

The problems were no less serious in Suffolk. Mr Edgar Granville, the Independent MP for Eye, told the Commons that of 238 houses in the village of Mendlesham, 224 shared public pumps and 208 families had to fetch and carry water over distances of from two hundred feet to a mile. At the village school 130 children had pail sewerage. He reported that the water supply had frequently failed during the previous twelve months. In the village of Thorndon in East Suffolk there were one hundred inhabitants and only three pumps, and many had to walk two hundred yards to fill their pails. They also had to use earth closets and in a few cases to share them with neighbours. Yet close at hand, in the same areas, military camps had been built during the war with water, sewerage and electricity.

These examples were typical of the general situation. Most parish, rural and district councils had begun to explore the scale of their local problems well before 1945, some before 1939, and now they were shocked to discover how the estimated costs had escalated. A sewerage scheme for Aylsham scheduled to cost £27,600 in 1939, was now going to cost £91,500.

The councils employed consulting engineers to prepare schemes, and in some cases gave such schemes early approval. Thus Thingoe Rural District Council adopted in January, and sent forward for county council and Ministry of Health approval, a comprehensive water scheme for the rural districts of Thingoe and Thedwastre and for the improvement of supplies in the borough of Bury St Edmunds. It involved 191 miles of mains. The provisional estimate of the cost was £352,000 at 1939 prices.

During the next few months schemes came forward thick and fast. In February Melford RDC considered a scheme to run a £300,000 trunk sewer along the Stour Valley from Clare, and invited Sudbury Borough Council to participate. Gipping RDC considered a scheme to give practically every parish in its area a piped water supply. Wells UDC approved a scheme for mains sewerage. In March Depwade RDC approved a £223,000 water supply project and Wayland RDC a £175,000 scheme. When the West Suffolk County Council approved the schemes for the Clare, Thingoe and Thedwastre areas in March, it was told that they would cost £500,000 — half the sum likely to be required for water schemes in West Suffolk as a whole.

It was obvious that these various schemes needed co-ordination. In Norfolk a "water conference" met and set up a representative county committee of engineers

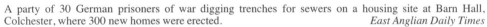

A party of 30 German prisoners of war digging trenches for sewers on a housing site at Barn Hall, Colchester, where 300 new homes were erected.   *East Anglian Daily Times*

to give advice. Similarly in East Suffolk members and officers of the County Council and all the rural district councils in its area formed an Advisory Committee for Rural Development at a conference in Ipswich in April, and decided to employ consulting engineers.

By this time the government was taking an initiative. The Commons gave a third reading in May to a Water Bill empowering the Minister of Health to secure a supply of piped water wherever it was needed, and enlarging the powers and duties of local authorities. The Bill set up a Central Water Committee to advise the government and local joint advisory water committees to plan ahead to meet the future needs of their areas. This measure gave a fillip to the improvement programme and those local authorities who had been holding back moved into action. Water supply and sewerage schemes, involving many miles of distribution and branch mains, were prepared throughout the eastern region and submitted for Ministry approval.

The bigger communities produced ambitious overall long-term development plans. "Plan for Norwich"—described as a fifty-year scheme for the city's development—had been in preparation over a period of two years. Its authors were two town planners, Mr C. H. James and Mr S. Rowland Pierce, who earlier had been the architects of the new City Hall. Their plan envisaged better roads— including a new inner ring road following the line of the old city wall and a new line for the outer ring road, construction of which had begun but been left unfinished before the war. The plan suggested that twenty-two thousand new houses would be required, not because of an increase in population but to provide satisfactory living conditions for everyone. It proposed more convenient shopping facilities and it outlined the provision considered necessary for industry. James assured the City Council when it formally received the plan on 30th May that all its proposals could be carried out "without undue disturbance or the destruction of the city's essential character".

In December Ipswich Town Council published details of a twenty-five year development plan for the town, providing for three ring roads—including a sixteen-mile-long parkway around the borough. It envisaged a town of 125,000 inhabitants and planned for ten thousand new houses—six thousand built by the Council and four thousand by private enterprise. The plan offered four alternative projects for a new civic centre and provided for four new swimming pools. It was to be exhibited and public reaction gathered before it was put before the Town Council early in 1946.

Lowestoft Town Council adopted in principle in September a redevelopment plan for the central area of the town. It had four main features. Local traffic was to be taken out of the shopping area on a new through route; central areas which had been blitzed were to be used as sites for a new civic centre and a town park; and a large square—Station Place—was to be created outside a modernized central railway station. It was intended for realization over a period of twenty-five years.

Many institutions, companies and organizations had their own rebuilding problems. In Great Yarmouth the parish church of St Nicholas was a burnt-out shell as a result of German bombing, and the vicar outlined at the annual parochial meeting tentative rebuilding plans. Some of the reconstruction work begun in Norwich during the summer was by firms in the footwear industry. Licences were issued for the rebuilding and reconstruction of Messrs Edwards & Holmes' factory, which had been totally destroyed in the 1942 blitz; and for the repair of Messrs W. Hurrell's factory, which had been severely damaged. At the outbreak of war 2,100 young people had been employed in footwear factories in the city, but the labour force had fallen to 682. The factory rebuilding programme was greeted as "an important first step towards the rehabilitation of the city's staple industry", and the manufacturers professed themselves keen to recapture their former export trade.

The Norfolk and Norwich Hospital, which had found it impossible to improve or extend buildings and equipment during the war, now launched— jointly with other Norfolk voluntary hospitals—an appeal for four hundred thousand pounds to cover planned capital expenditure over the following five years. There was widespread concern that hospital provision in the region would be inadequate after derequisitioning of many large buildings that had been used during the war as hospital annexes: such buildings as the Leys School and the Examination Hall in Cambridge, Hintlesham Hall in Suffolk, and Giffords Hall— a thirteenth-century mansion at Stoke-by-Nayland in Essex. This forced a fundamental reassessment of each county's hospital needs.

The seaside resorts felt a special sense of urgency, for they hoped that the summer of 1945 would see a resumption of their holiday trade. In the early part of the year they fretted about hotels and boarding-houses still requisitioned, about defence works on their promenades and mines on their beaches. As we have seen, some progress was being made in these matters, but much remained to be done.

Easter brought hopeful signs; all bus services between Norwich and Yarmouth, Lowestoft and Cromer had to be duplicated to handle the weekend crowds. There were queues at the shops. The beaches were closed from sunset to sunrise by order of the military. The Mayor of Great Yarmouth opened the first conference staged in the town since 1940, welcoming the lead given by sixty delegates who had assembled to discuss the problems of the Licensed Victuallers.

The Pier Pavilion at Felixstowe was derequisitioned on 1st March and it was repaired and redecorated in time to have bands playing during a five-week season commencing on 29th July. Only a small section of the beach was reopened in time, but children played between the barbed wire defences that remained and deck-chairs were hired "wherever possible behind the defence barrier".

Great Yarmouth staged a ten-week summer season, opening at the end of June. A portion of the central beach between Britannia Pier and the Jetty and a portion of the Gorleston beach in the vicinity of the spur breakwater were reopened to the public. They were soon crowded, but no boats, chairs or tents were permitted on them. At the Wellington Pier Pavilion there was a Show Time concert party of seventeen artistes plus the resident orchestra; at the Winter Gardens there was Harry Roy's Tiger Raggamuffins dance band; and at the Marina was David Miller and his broadcasting orchestra of thirteen musicians.

Lowestoft opened the whole of the South Front to the public, cleaned up and restored its gardens and other amenities, and brought out a few bathing chalets, beach huts and deck chairs for Pakefield beach. But when the summer arrived lack of accommodation and facilities for visitors caused great concern in the resort. The Council received hundreds of letters each week asking for addresses of accommodation and found it impossible to respond. An estimated twenty-thousand visitors arrived in the town each week, most of them day-trippers, and those who failed to bring their own food found the few restaurants totally inadequate. Public houses sold out of beer in two days and closed for the rest of the week.

Other resorts progressed slowly back to some degree of normality. Beaches were progressively cleared and declared safe. At Southwold the public had access to about six hundred yards of sea-front—from the Pleasure Pier southwards to a point opposite East Cliff; the pier itself opened for the first time on August Bank Holiday. The beach at Cromer reopened late in August, as did all but a small section of the beach at Sheringham. Beaches opposite the fronts at Overstrand and Mundesley came back into use, but the beach between Sheringham and Weybourne was still dangerous. The regatta was revived at Blakeney "in miniature".

Despite everyone's best efforts, however, visitors slept in promenade shelters and on open beaches in several resorts during August—despite grey skies, chilly winds and intermittent heavy rain.

The Town Clerk of Lowestoft, Mr F. Nunney, was a member of a deputation which saw the Lord Privy Seal, Mr Arthur Greenwood, in November to present a case on behalf of fifty-one coastal resorts in the former defence evacuation areas. It urged the need for speedy restoration of damaged hotels and catering establishments and pleaded for financial assistance.

In all the ports there was frantic activity after VE-Day to return to normal peacetime operations, with particular concern to see a resumption of fishing. At Great Yarmouth the Navy released sufficient of the requisitioned premises to meet the needs of the Port and Haven Commissioners, but because revenue had been reduced during the war the piers and some quays had become dilapidated. Lighting on the quays and under the Herring Market required a complete overhaul and the water supply at the fish wharf had been discontinued owing to age and defects beyond repair, so that the quays and markets had no means of washing down. To cope with this last need the Commissioners brought surplus pumps from the National Fire Service.

Work began in May to reconvert for fishing twenty-eight of the East Anglian

A busy scene on the fish wharf at Great Yarmouth on 31st October when drifters arrived to unload herrings.
Eastern Daily Press

vessels which had been requisitioned by the Royal Navy. They were stripped of their guns, asdic and sweeping gear, refitted, given back their trawls and returned to their peacetime owners. As for the others, there was simply a promise that they would be released "as soon as operational requirements permit".

The first trawlers were fishing from Lowestoft in mid-June, and the fleet was built up steadily week by week. By mid-July there was already a regular daily landing sufficient to supply the shops of Norfolk and Suffolk; on the 16th, for example, six vessels delivered one hundred tons at Lowestoft.

The first drift fishing from Yarmouth and Lowestoft since 1939 began on 15th October. Before the war up to one thousand drifters had landed their catches at these two ports, but in 1945 the number was well under two hundred. Lowestoft, which itself had once had a fleet of two hundred, sent only twenty. Yarmouth sent twelve, compared with a pre-war fleet of just under one hundred.

About 130 vessels came from Scotland to work from the two ports, with more than a thousand Scottish fishermen. A committee of Scots regulated the landings. They decided to maintain a tradition of spending Saturday night and Sunday in port, although the Yarmouth and Lowestoft men wanted to work to full capacity in

The crew of a Scottish drifter clearing nets at Great Yarmouth.   *Eastern Daily Press*

response to an appeal by the Minister of Agriculture and Fisheries that every herring possible should be caught.

A few Scottish fishergirls arrived in Yarmouth and Lowestoft at the beginning of October to gut and barrel the cure, as they had always done in pre-war years, but their numbers were restricted because of difficulties in finding them accommodation.

The October full moon controlled the swarming of the herring and the start of the voyage, and in 1945 this fell a little later than usual, on 21st October. After that the fish trains rolled out of Yarmouth and Lowestoft every afternoon just as in pre-war days, giving next-morning deliveries via London, Peterborough and York to the south-west, the Midlands and the north. Fish seemed scarce during the first few weeks, but by early November the fish trains built up to 120 vans each day.

The Ministry controlled prices. Herring were sold to the home market at prices ranging from eighty seven shillings minimum to ninety-one shillings maximum a cran. (A cran was a basket measure holding anything from 1,200 to 2,000 herring, according to their size. The general rule was that a cran would fill a barrel for despatch, but this was not invariably so.) When market prices fell below eighty-seven shillings the fish went automatically to the curers who sold to the Ministry of Food at agreed prices. This happened for the first time on 2nd

117

November and the Scottish girls went to work after several weeks of enforced idleness.

There were good landings during November—4,873 crans at Great Yarmouth and 1,400 crans at Lowestoft on the 15th, when the Scots girls had plenty left over for curing; 5,825 crans at Yarmouth and 3,900 at Lowestoft on the 20th, the night of the full moon. By the 23rd, however, the landings were much reduced and Scottish drifters were beginning to leave Lowestoft. There was no curing during the last week of November and the curers and their staffs departed.

It was then announced that the season's total catch was 88,136 crans at Yarmouth and 57,511 crans at Lowestoft. The total cure between the two ports had been twenty thousand barrels, whereas the Ministry of Food had been hoping for two hundred thousand barrels for transmission to the United Nations Relief and Rehabilitation Agency (UNRRA) to help alleviate the food problem in Europe.

Two developments during the season presaged big changes in the industry. A new process of brine-freezing was introduced at two new freezing plants, one at Yarmouth and one at Lowestoft. The herring were processed by quick freezing, then boxed and transferred to cold store. Another new machine brought into use experimentally at Great Yarmouth used conveyor-belt techniques to gut ninety herring a minute, compared to the twenty-six to thirty-six a minute the Scots fishergirls could handle.

The appearance of a machine which could gut herrings at the rate of 90 per minute suggested that there were big changes ahead for the East Coast fishing industry.   *Eastern Daily Press*

Swedish timber ship Alstern docked at Kings Lynn, the first foreign cargo ship there since the outbreak of war. *Eastern Daily Press*

Other trade began to return to the ports. Sixty-five merchant vessels, of 11,256 registered tons, entered Great Yarmouth harbour during June, two-thirds of them laden, the others in ballast or coming for repairs. In June timber ships from Scandinavia were seen again at the quays: first the Swedish steamship *Asloeg* in Great Yarmouth and soon afterwards others bringing Baltic timber to King's Lynn and Lowestoft.

The London and North Eastern Railway Company, which operated services from Harwich to the Continent, announced that it would build two new passenger ships and three train ferries for the route. The service from Parkeston Quay to the Hook of Holland was reintroduced with a night sailing by the SS *Prague* on Wednesday, 14th November, and a weekly service from Harwich to the Danish port of Esbjerg on the night of 12th December by the MS *Parkeston*.

Early in the year Norfolk County Council called a conference of delegates representative of all interests in Broadland— public, private and commercial—to discuss how best "to preserve and improve the general amenities of the rivers and broads of Norfolk and Suffolk". At the time some of the Broads were still mined and staked. The possibility that Broadland might become a national park was raised by one speaker, and a committee was set up to investigate and report.

Many sporting activities had maintained a tenuous continuity during the war years, and their devotees were impatient to resume full-time activity. Norwich City and Ipswich Town football clubs both faced formidable financial problems. Norwich had had a large deficit in 1939 which had increased in the war years, during which the club had managed to have extensive work done on its ground, levelling and returfing the pitch and repainting the stand and dressing rooms. Shareholders met in August and heard that the bank overdraft was over eleven thousand pounds, outstanding loans totalled £11,990, and there were debts of £5,795.

Ipswich had similar problems. The chairman of the club, Mr Philip Cobbold, announced in March that at least £7,500 was required to get it going again but the directors' efforts to raise this amount by an issue of debentures had produced only four thousand pounds. Further efforts were made, and Mr Cobbold was able to confirm in May that the club would restart football at Portman Road.

At the annual meeting in London in July the Football League decided to play regionally during what was to be regarded as a transitional season. Transport was still difficult and clubs preferred a competition which could be fulfilled with one-day journeys out and home. The Third Division South was divided into two groups, and for the first half of the season Norwich and Ipswich were members of a group of eleven clubs, the others being Southend, Mansfield, Port Vale, Notts County, Walsall, Northampton, Watford, Clapton Orient and Queen's Park Rangers.

The season opened on 25th August. Watford visited Carrow Road, and Ipswich played away against Port Vale. A crowd of 8,186 saw Norwich run up an 8–1 victory, but Ipswich lost 2–3. Norwich City's second fixture was an evening match against Port Vale at Carrow Road, which the visitors won 4–3. Once the season was under way attendances at home games topped eleven thousand, and for a match against Ipswich Town on 1st December it was 16,301. Ipswich had a more difficult start. After losing to Port Vale in their away game, the following week they played them again in their first League match at Portman Road for six years before a crowd of twelve thousand; Port Vale beat them again, 1–0[1].

Queen's Park Rangers ran out top of the table, with Norwich second. At home on Christmas Day before a crowd of 20,082 Norwich forced a draw, but in the away game on Boxing Day they lost 2–1.

As the year ended men and women were returning in large numbers from the services and the war industries to their regular jobs in factory, field and fishing-boat; new homes and new amenities to provide more comfortable living conditions were in prospect; and there was leisure again and a chance to relax at seaside and sports ground. The foundations of a new post-war society were being energetically laid down.

CHAPTER TEN

Attitudes And Aspirations

SOME THINGS are measurable, and some are not. It was possible to list the practical tasks of reconstruction and regeneration that faced British society when the war had ended. It was possible to assess the physical and economic resources that might be made available. What was impossible to quantify, but equally important, was the spirit of the people. What attitudes did they bring to the challenges of peace-time, what aspirations, and what degree of determination to fulfil them?

The outcome of the general election in 1945 offered important evidence on this matter. Labour had gained a dramatic victory, and it had done so on a policy which emphasized "social justice". The fact was that all parties agreed on this concept, which had been popularized by the publication in December 1942 of the Beveridge Report, a document setting out guidelines for a welfare state. Beveridge argued the case for full employment, a minimum subsistence level for all, special allowances for dependent children and health care financed by the state. This plan was sponsored and accepted by the Churchill coalition government which in February, before the war had ended, made a start towards its implementation with a Family Allowance Bill to provide five shillings a week for every child in a family except the first. Notwithstanding this gesture of good intentions, the electorate decided that it trusted Labour to implement the full Beveridge programme rather than the coalition.

There was a belief in the value of collective action, not only in the political field. During the war years team spirit rather than individual initiative had been encouraged, and out of this necessity an instinct for co-operation and comradeship had developed. These were seen as virtues to be encouraged in the changed circumstances of peacetime.

The Home Guard had developed its own special ethos, and many of its members were loath to surrender it when the force was disbanded. A Home Guard Club was opened at Colman House in Norwich, one of its founders declaring: "The comradeship and friendship that developed in the war years must not be allowed to disappear". Ex-members of the Cambridge Home Guard formed an Old Comrades Association in that area, and similar action was taken elsewhere.

A meeting in Beccles in September decided that the town's war memorial should take the form of a club were ex-service personnel could meet to keep alive the fellowship they had felt when away from their homes.

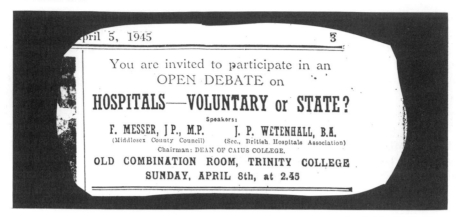

Cambridge Daily News

There was an element of idealism at work, but it found expression in severely practical proposals. And it was not confined to those who had been in uniform. The Mass Observation organization questioned civilian residents of East Anglia about the form of memorial they would consider appropriate to the sacrifice of those who had died in the war. A typical response was: "No statues, but things of lasting value, such as parks, hospitals or additions to them."[1] There was much evidence that this represented the general view. At Southwold a public meeting a few weeks after VE-Day voted that the town's war memorial should be a new forty-bed hospital costing forty thousand pounds, and at Fakenham too a public meeting decided in principle on a war memorial hospital.

People looked for more than fraternity in a social sense; they wanted it to extend to community care for those with special problems or special needs. They looked for a better quality of life *for everyone* than many, particularly the unemployed and the sick, had experienced during the nineteen-thirties. Another respondent to the Mass Observation questionnaire declared: "What I want is work and wages for the living, and a democratic and Christian country."[2] An example of the prevalent attitude was provided by the Great Yarmouth Social Welfare Committee (metamorphozed from the earlier Public Assistance Committee), which resolved to increase Christmas relief given to all adults on its register from five to seven shillings and refused to be deterred when the Town Clerk suggested this was too generous and warned that the committee's members might be surcharged.

The Labour government's first budget—introduced in the Commons in October by Dr Hugh Dalton, Chancellor of the Exchequer—had a redistributive flavour. Two million people with low incomes were taken out of tax altogether by an increase in the exemption limit, and everyone derived some benefit from increased personal allowances. Taxable income was assessed in three bands: the first fifty pounds was taxed at fifteen per cent, the next seventy-five pounds at thirty per cent and the remainder at forty-five per cent. This latter represented a reduction of five per cent on the wartime rate of tax, but the reduction was delayed until April 1946. These reductions were balanced by increases in the rates of surtax paid by those with high incomes; this became fifty-five per cent on the first five hundred pounds in excess of two thousand pounds a year, rising to a maximum of 92.5 per cent on incomes in excess of twenty thousand pounds. The budget also abolished purchase tax on a number of household utensils and fittings.

Any government would have operated within severe limitations at this time. The immense war effort had overstretched the British economy and left the nation bankrupt. Many of the dreams of a brave new world had to be placed in cold storage.

Through the later years of the war Britain had been living on goods and materials supplied by the United States on the basis of Lend-Lease. This meant that, at least in theory, they could be returned later—as indeed some warships were—or that, as in the case of food, settlement of the bill could be postponed. On 24th August President Truman announced abruptly the ending of Lend-Lease. Professor Maynard Keynes, one of Britain's leading economists, was at once sent to Washington to seek some new dollar credit arrangement. After twelve weeks' negotiation the United States granted Britain a loan of $3,750 million on which it could draw for six years, with interest at two per cent. The loan was to be repaid in fifty annual instalments, the first on 31st November 1951. Many in Britain found it difficult to accept the reality of Britain's stark situation and *The Times* greeted the agreement as "an economic Dunkirk".

Against this background the new Prime Minister, Clement Attlee, told the Trades Union Congress in Blackpool in September that he could hold out no hope of great improvements in the near future. "The position is not going to be easy in the testing time ahead" he said. The United Kingdom had drawn heavily on its social capital during the war, there was a world food shortage and, "with the best will in the world we cannot overtake the housing shortage for months and years to come".

Despite the difficulties investment in the nation's infrastructure was put in hand. The people of Ipswich saw tangible evidence of this as three 320–foot chimneys rose to change the skyline at Cliff Quay. They were part of a new power station which was scheduled to feed electricity into the national grid from 1947. When completed, at a cost of £8,250,000, it was to have 270,000-kilowatt capacity. Immediately, it provided jobs for three hundred construction workers.

East Suffolk announced a programme of new road construction during the years 1946–50, to cost over three million pounds, and similar planning was under way throughout the region by the year-end. The provision of jobs was everywhere a major anxiety and capital projects such as these offered some reassurance. Cambridge Trades Council and Labour Party called for twelve thousand new jobs in its area, and urged the government to encourage the establishment of light industries in Cambridge.

The government had an agenda of its own, as had been set out in its election manifesto. First it introduced a Bill to nationalize the Bank of England, which the Commons approved on a second reading by 348 votes to 153. Three weeks later—in November—the Leader of the House, Mr Herbert Morrison, told MPs that coal, gas, electricity, the railways, canals, road services and dock and harbour undertakings would also be nationalized. Labour argued that these industries represented the economic foundation of society, provided the essential services and facilitated the creation of national wealth, and that therefore they should be owned and operated in the interests of society as a whole, not for the benefit of individual shareholders. The Conservative opposition pledged dogged opposition arguing that individual enterprise would produce greater benefit for all.

The special interest of many in the eastern counties was in the future of agriculture. A first concern of many farmers was to regain possession of, and to return to production, land that had been taken by the Services during the war. Under constant pressure by eastern counties MPs, progress was made. By the autumn 7,700 of the forty thousand acres requisitioned in Norfolk had been returned, and most of it was being farmed again. There was no sign, however, that the large area near Thetford taken for use as a battle school would soon be handed back*.

When the pressures of wartime were relaxed some farmers, particularly in Suffolk, showed a nostalgic hankering after the old ways. Their attitude was probably accounted for by the limited size of their farms—they averaged only eighty-two acres. And, although their sheep population had declined, there was still a strong desire to maintain mixed farming.

It was clear to the most conservative farmers, however, that they could not revert to a pre-war pattern. A great deal of land had been properly drained for the first time during the war, and this improvement had illuminated the scale of the work still needed. Although one hundred thousand acres had been drained in Suffolk, there were four hundred thousand more acres requiring attention.

The war had brought a big increase in the use of farm machinery. In 1939 there had been sixty thousand tractors at work in Britain; there were now nearly three times as many. Pre-war single-furrow ploughs had almost disappeared, having been replaced by two-, three-and four-furrow ploughs. There were now two and a half thousand combine harvesters, an increase of 150 per cent since 1942[3]. Not everyone was enthusiastic about the machines. The *East Anglian Daily Times* farming correspondent Lavengro wrote: "Several well-known East

---

*In 1950 land in the Stanford Principal Training Area was compulsorily purchased by the Ministry of Defence, which indicated its intention to retain it in perpetuity.

Suffolk farmers I met on the Corn Market on Tuesday were unalterably opposed to using combines." He agreed with them:

> While combines have their advantages by early in-gathering, will they compensate for the inevitable loss in price, as is predicted with barley gluts? More is available than either maltster or merchant can conveniently deal with; hence the maximum price is not obtainable . . .

The feeling for the farm horse persisted strongly, as was demonstrated by three Suffolk Horse Society shows during 1945, which attracted big entries and record attendances.

The Suffolk Agricultural Association's County Show in Christchurch Park, Ipswich, during the summer was the first since 1939 and the only county agricultural show held in Britain during 1945. Thousands attended, and the 723 entries came from all over Suffolk, Norfolk and Essex. Large crowds gathered at the grand ring to watch hunters jumping hurdles, all the traditional country crafts were displayed at booths and stalls, and the band of the Royal Marines (HMS *Ganges*) provided the music.

Farm employees were concerned about wages and working conditions. Until 1939 they had suffered low wages and low status in the labour market. During the

More than 220 horses were entered at Wymondham Horse Show on 15th September. Picture shows the winning team leading a parade of horses.　　　　　　　　　　　　　　　*Eastern Daily Press*

war their thinking had been transformed; they had become aware of their importance to the national economy and with this had come a belief in the value of trade unionism and a build-up of organized strength in the National Union of Agricultural Workers. Nearly 1,700 new members were recruited in Norfolk during 1944, and in Suffolk the number of union branches increased by nearly fifty per cent during the first nine months of 1945.

The union sought a substantial improvement in pay and working conditions. In January 1945 the Agricultural Wages Board in London awarded an increase of five shillings a week to adult male farm workers of twenty-one and over, bringing their minimum to £3 10s, but it awarded no increase to female and juvenile workers. The Union was dissatisfied. It demanded a minimum wage of £4 10s a week.

During the war the farmers had regularly demanded a direct link between wage costs and farm product prices, and had equally regularly been refused. Because of this Suffolk farmers were indignant about any wage increases, while Norfolk farmers demanded that they must be linked to an increase in cereal prices. When new farm prices were announced in March, however, there was no change in payment for cereals. There were increases for potatoes and sugar beet, and the Norfolk NFU secretary thought "the overall increase of national farm revenue will entitle the government to feel that they have met the claim".

The Labour government's agricultural policy was announced by the new minister, Mr Tom Williams, in the Commons in November. He promised a permanent system of assured markets and guaranteed prices for principal products. There would be an annual price review for cereals, potatoes and sugar beet, and prices for crops would be fixed eighteen months ahead of harvest. In the case of livestock, milk and eggs, minimum prices would be fixed for overlapping four-year periods, with biennial review. To promote maximum efficiency, committees similar to the County War Agricultural Executive Committees would be constituted on a permanent basis.

There had been considerable apprehension about Labour's plans in agriculture. The farmers had hoped for a removal of wartime controls and committees, but neutral voices had warned them before the change of government that that was unrealistic, as in this leading article in the *East Anglian Daily Times:*

> While there are some elements in the farming fraternity who argue that they should be allowed their old independence, there are many more who realise that conditions in the postwar period will be such that none of us will be able to conduct our affairs without taking into consideration the over-riding needs and claims of others. While British agriculture continues to receive financial help from the National Exchequer a certain measure of control is inevitable.

Now that Labour's plans were known another regional newspaper, the *Eastern Daily Press*, offered the opinion that assured markets and guaranteed prices would "put an end to the uncertainty about the future place of the agricultural industry in the national economy", and it added: "That this procedure must be linked up with a system of wage regulation and also with some means of assuring that the land is being used to its maximum capacity of production is inevitable."

The National Farmers' Union thought the government statement of policy "a statesmanlike effort which, if developed realistically in concert with the industry, will take British agriculture well on the way towards its goal of full and permanent service to the nation". Farmers' spokesmen in East Anglia were less generous. Mr. J. F. Wright, the Norfolk NFU secretary, thought that permanent control by committees was "a bitter pill".

Millions of women had served in the armed forces, Civil Defence services, on farms and in factories, and their experiences had significantly influenced their outlook on society and their role in it. Soon after the general election a Status of Women Campaign Committee rallied over a thousand, including many new women MPs, to the Central Hall at Westminster. This gathering delivered an ultimatum to the government that it must take "active steps to establish their right to equality with men". One of the new Norwich MPs, Lady Noel-Buxton, was the first speaker. She began:

> I hope that there will never again be a meeting of this kind. I am determined to do everything possible to make it as ridiculous to hold a meeting to consider the status of women as it would be to hold a meeting to consider the status of men.

In the eastern counties women had made their voices heard. Cambridge, Norwich and Ipswich had established Women Citizens' Associations. Cambridge for only the third time in its history had elected a woman Mayor, Lady Bragg. There were many indications, however, that women would need to do more to establish their claims to equality. A Texan who spent an extended period as a visiting professor at Cambridge wrote in the *Saturday Evening Post* an enthusiastic eulogy of the town and its people after his return home, but he predicted that the University would have to change greatly its attitude to women if they were to enjoy any sort of equality. And when early in 1945 the Reverend W. Hargrave Thomas argued at a meeting of East Suffolk Education Committee for the principle of equal pay for equal work for men and women teachers of the same professional status, only four of his colleagues supported him. Seven voted against the proposition and several others abstained.

Despite the reservations and hesitations, despite the economic restraints and despite the ideological differences between the political parties, there was optimism in the post-war world. There was great faith in the benefits of science and technology. The *East Anglian Daily Times* acknowledged that scientists and research workers could help with advice to farmers through the new farming institutes. It headlined the news that America had produced an atomic bomb:

MANKIND'S TREMENDOUS NEW SOURCES OF POWER
ATOM BOMB REVELATION THE WORLD'S TALKING-POINT

Scientists and Industrial Revolution

"Substitute for Fuels and Electric Power"

Not all expectations were realized. Among planned improvements that were postponed was the raising of the school-leaving age to fifteen. There was insufficient school accommodation to fulfil the policy that had been agreed by the coalition government, and so it was to be delayed until April 1947. As the year ended the idea was voiced in some quarters that a large number of small village schools would have to be closed.

Cambridge University, when the students returned in October, functioned under difficulties. Whole blocks of university accommodation was still under government requisition and colleges urgently needed more of their tutors to be released from the forces. There were only three thousand undergraduates, no more than in the last year of war, whereas in a normal pre-war year there would have been about 5,300. A gradual influx from the services was expected over the first six months, however, and it was thought probable that the total might grow to six thousand by 1947. The women's colleges had rather more than their normal five hundred pre-war total. "College tutors are being bombarded daily by letters and telephone calls with requests for admission", it was stated in September.

And how did this new generation of undergraduates feel about their world? When the Union Society resumed its debates, it voted on 12th November, "that this house has no confidence in H.M. Government", and on 26th November "that Great Britain has taken the road to serfdom".

Right-wing critics also attacked the British Broadcasting Corporation which was arguably one of the major educational influences of the time. The BBC's charter was due for renewal in 1946 and Mr Somerset de Chair, while MP for South-West Norfolk, wrote to *The Times* alleging that the Corporation was "a Frankenstein's monster which is getting out of control". Most Conservatives were convinced, he said, that the whole bias of the BBC was towards the left. It should be made to face "the blast of healthy competition". Soon after this declaration, however, Mr de Chair faced the electorate—and lost his seat in Parliament.

Most people's complaint about the BBC was that they could not hear enough of it. Long before the war there had been concern about the poor quality of radio reception in East Anglia, and the Corporation had promised a regional station "as soon as practicable". Hopes ran high but as the war ended the Ministry of Information announced that at that time it was considered impracticable. "There will be great disappointment", the *Eastern Daily Press* declared in a leading article.

Most people still relied upon sound radio. There were only twenty-three thousand television sets in the United Kingdom, and no programmes had been transmitted during the war years. The BBC announced that transmissions would be resumed at Alexandra Palace in the spring of 1946, and this news was followed by a demonstration by Pye in a Cambridge studio of "a revolutionary new television system" which could use a single transmitter for sound and picture.

There was a perceptible boost to cultural activity of all kinds. A group in Ipswich campaigned for a repertory theatre in the town and appealed for three thousand pounds towards the initial capital cost. They envisaged a four-hundred seat theatre in the Old Tower Street cinema.

Considerable regional pride was shown in a new British opera, *Peter Grimes,* because it had been composed by a thirty-one-year-old son of Lowestoft, Mr Benjamin Britten. It had its first performance at Sadler's Wells Theatre in London in June, marking the theatre's reopening after more than four years in darkness. The performers included Peter Pears in the title role, Joan Cross, Edith Coates and Roderick Jones. It received an enthusiastic reception and Britten took his bow after seven curtain calls. The *East Anglian Daily Times* kept the folk back in Suffolk well informed:

> The libretto is based on a work by the Rev George Crabbe, the Suffolk poet of more than a century ago, and its subject is a grim story of the hard life of the old time Suffolk coast fisherman . . . Mr Britten's score is of the modern school of music. It implies a break with many of the time-honoured conventions and traditions of the foreign operas, and offers instead an approach to reality and a genius for the construction of swift-moving and enthralling drama. The writing is immensely vigorous and the complex and brilliant orchestration reveals originality and inventive powers of an exceptional kind.

Flatford Mill, childhood home of John Constable and subject of some of his best-known paintings, was established as a pioneer field studies centre. The National Trust offered the use of the building, which had been placed in its custody, and the Carnegie Trust gave two thousand pounds to the Council for the Promotion of Field Studies to help meet the cost of adaptation and equipment.

Colour and ceremony were reinstituted wherever possible, and this spread some cheer in what were still austere times. No one succeeded better in this regard than the new Lord Mayor of Norwich when he revived the traditional civic reception at the Castle Museum in November. Wearing his black and gold robes and gold chain of office and with the Lady Mayoress at his side, he took up position in the Keep before the bearers of the sword of state, the two castle maces and the two gilt maces. The orchestra of the Royal Norfolk Regiment played in the gallery. Footmen in livery announced the arriving guests: members and officials of the City Council, magistrates, and representatives of the clergy and of the professional and business life of the city. Seventy per cent of those present wore evening dress—not much seen during the war. One who was present declared, "There was a strong smell of mothballs."

Other elected bodies did their best. The Town Council at Great Yarmouth, for example, collected its civic regalia from the Birmingham vaults in which it had been stored during the war and displayed it behind the Mayor's chair at a July meeting, for the first time since 1939.

Civic pride had survived undiminished, but it was coupled now with a wider vision. The people of East Anglia had met and mixed with visitors from all over the world; many men and some women from the eastern counties had travelled over the farthest horizons. The idea of international goodwill had been actively encouraged by gestures such as that of 2nd Air Division of the US Air Force, which had subscribed twenty thousand pounds to provide a library and museum in Norwich presenting the history and achievements of American units which had flown from local bases. A Norwich school-teacher wrote: "If anyone were to suggest that the Norwich war memorial should be a sum of money for travelling, I should subscribe willingly. I think travel is important for future international relationships . . ."[4]. A Suffolk lady suggested "some organisation which would help to increase man's consciousness of world unity and brotherhood. I would suggest a travelling fund."[5]

The League of Nations, a product of the First World War, was replaced in 1945 by the United Nations Organization. From the early days of the war Britain and her allies and "associated nations"—which included the United States—had referred to themselves as the United Nations, and in September 1944 a conference at Dumbarton Oaks, near Washington, floated the idea of an international peace-keeping organization which would be able to take military action if necessary where a threat to peace was discerned. A formal decision to set up such an organization was made at the Yalta conference, and fifty national delegations met in San Francisco on 25th April 1945 to create the UNO. Mr Anthony Eden led the UK delegation and Mr Clement Attlee, not yet Prime Minister, was another member. In June the conference unanimously adopted a world Security Charter, which made the maintenance of peace the responsibility of a Security Council on which each of the five great powers—Britain, the United States, Russia, France and China—would have a permanent seat and an effective veto. The first Assembly of the United Nations Organization was fixed for January 1946, and was to take place in London.

In East Anglia internationalists were ahead of events. Local branches of the League of Nations Union, a comparable organization created after the world war of 1914–18, were active from the beginning of the year. The annual meeting of the Cambridge branch in February, presided over by the Mayor, Mr. G. Wilding, resolved to work hard to focus public debate on the proposals for a new peace organization (see advert). There were, of course, some sceptics; but the Cambridge University Union Society was out of tune with public opinion when it refused to give approval to "the organisation and policy of the United Nations". It sat on the fence, voting 104–104. The chairman gave a casting vote for the motion.

Circumstances did not look propitious. Early efforts by the Big Three leaders at their Yalta meeting to agree the future shape of Europe had ended in mutual suspicion. Churchill came away from Yalta believing that he had achieved a compromise agreement about the future of Poland, the nation for whose independence and integrity Britain had gone to war in the first place. But within weeks non-

THE RECENT
'DUMBARTON OAKS' CONFERENCE
VITALLY CONCERNS
YOU
AND
YOUR FAMILY
Come and hear all about the United Nations
Plans from
LORD LYTTON
at the
GUILDHALL
MONDAY, FEB. 26th, 8.0 p.m,
Doors open 7.30 p.m. Organ
Chairman: HIS WORSHIP THE MAYOR
(Councillor G. Wilding)

LEAGUE OF NATIONS UNION AND C.U.S.I.A.

communist Polish leaders who went under safe conduct to consult with Soviet officers were arrested and taken as prisoners to Moscow, and there were reports that four thousand Poles had been arrested and deported to labour camps in the Soviet Union[6]. A new kind of "cold war" seemed to be beginning.

Churchill faced much criticism in the Commons. From the Labour side Mr Arthur Greenwood declared that "it was foreign to the principles of British justice for the fate of a nation to be decided in its absence and behind its back". Twenty-five Conservative MPs refused to support the government in a vote; one of the most outspoken was Lord Dunglass, Conservative MP for Lanark*; and another was the Norwich MP, Mr Henry Strauss, who resigned his post as Parliamentary Secretary to the Minister of Town and Country Planning because he "found it impossible to approve of the treatment of the Polish people by the Crimea conference".

By early April Churchill had become fearful that what was happening in Poland presaged similar problems elsewhere in eastern Europe. He telephoned General Eisenhower, the Supreme Commander, and told him: "I deem it highly

*Later he became Prime Minister, as Sir Alec Douglas Home.

131

important that we should shake hands with the Russians as far to the east as possible."[7] Eisenhower, however, agreed with the Soviet High Command that he would not move on Berlin, but rather to the south and east, and a little later he informed them that US forces would not advance beyond the area of Linz.

At this juncture President Roosevelt died suddenly, and Churchill could only appeal to the newly installed President Truman to instruct Eisenhower to go on to Prague. Truman replied that he would leave tactical deployment to the military[8]. In the north, British troops saw that Churchill's wishes were met, for—as related in an earlier chapter—they raced to the Baltic and prevented a Red Army advance into Schleswig–Holstein and, possibly, Denmark.

These problems and anxieties were kept from the public, but the commanding officers of US air bases in East Anglia knew that events were not unfolding as satisfactorily as official pronouncements suggested. Three days after VE-Day the US 8th Air Force was placed on alert. Its officers were given to understand that they might have to undertake a mission to Berlin because the Russians had taken control of areas which it had been agreed should be occupied by British and American forces.

Some at least of the US commanding officers believed they would be required to attack the Red Army if it did not withdraw. The 390th Bomb Group at Framlingham understood that it would be the lead unit, and that there would be a massive task force 145 miles long. Eighteen US fighter groups of Mustangs were also alerted. At the last moment President Truman aborted the operation*.

Thus at the moment of victory in the war there were serious tensions between the nations which had been allies. On 4th May Churchill telegraphed his wife, who was in Moscow, that "beneath these triumphs lie poisonous politics and deadly international rivalries"[9].

The aftermath of this situation confronted the new British Prime Minister, Mr Clement Attlee, at another Big Three conference, at Potsdam in July. This ended with a declaration that understanding between the three governments had improved, and it created a Council of Foreign Ministers to prepare settlements for "a just and enduring peace".

---

*In a letter to Ian Hawkins dated 26th June, 1991 from the then CO of the 390th Bomb Group, Joseph A Moller, stated: "Regarding the mission which was set for three days after VE Day and later scrubbed, you will note in the article I stated that I discussed this scrubbing of the mission at Orlando where the 8th A.F. Historical Society met and that a reporter tried to confirm the story. I told him to call Jimmy Doolittle, which he did, and Jimmy told him that Joseph Moller is a truthful man and if he told you this it is the truth. That is the only time I have discussed the mission publicly . . . When I had the privilege of discussing this question with General Eisenhower some years later when he was Chief of Staff, we agreed that if we had flown the mission and displayed the 8th Air Force strength, we probably would not have had to bomb the Russians. It should be noted that the Russians did not begin their advance until after 9.00 that morning, obviously waiting to see what the reaction of the Americans was going to be, and when the Americans did not react, the world saw armed Russian troops advancing and American troops retreating. The net result of his scrubbing of the mission also necessitated the Berlin air lift because the Russians had taken control of a large industrial section, part of which was to be occupied by England and part by the U.S. in accordance with the agreement for the occupation of Germany."

The Council of Foreign Ministers held its first meeting in London in September. It failed to agree on interpretation of the agreements reached at Potsdam, disagreed about the nature of the regimes installed in eastern Europe, and was unable even to agree on the terms of a communique. Its talks were abruptly suspended. It tried again in December, this time in Moscow, and reached some measure of agreement; but Mr Ernest Bevin, the British Foreign Secretary, guardedly summed up: "It achieved what was humanly possible under present circumstances, and its actual significance depends on implementation of the agreements reached."

If ideas about the future of eastern Europe caused discord, at least there was agreement on what should be done with Germany. It was to be completely disarmed and demilitarized and divided into occupation zones: one for each of the Big Three victors and one for France. Germans whose pre-war homes had been in parts of Poland, Czechoslovakia and Hungary were to be expelled. Nazis were to be removed from posts of public responsibility, and German war criminals were to be brought to trial. Twenty-two leading Nazis—including Goering, Hess and Admiral Donitz—faced a War Crimes Tribunal in Nuremberg in November, accused of "crimes against humanity". This trial continued for almost a year.

It was principally in western Europe that there appeared to be opportunities for constructive work. Its starving population required relief, and the people of East Anglia played an active role. A "Save Europe Now" organization was set up and one of its first big public meetings was held in the Stuart Hall in Norwich in November. The Lord Mayor presided and was supported on the platform by the Bishop of Norwich and the Ipswich MP, Richard Stokes, who was the principal speaker. Earlier, in the Commons, Mr Stokes had asked the Minister of Food if he was "aware of the consternation felt by a large number of people in this country at his decision to increase the general ration at Christmas while Europe starves". The Minister replied that his first duty was to the British public.

The Norwich meeting collected the signatures of those who said they would forego their Christmas extras if the food went to Europe. In Cambridge a fund to help alleviate famine in Europe was launched at a public meeting called by representative undergraduate societies and a committee representing local churches; it was chaired by the Mayor, Lady Bragg, The large gathering was told by the Bishop of Ely, Dr Harold E. Wynn, that no words could describe the intensity of suffering, starvation, want and destitution that the coming winter might bring to millions in Europe. He urged people to accept more readily and uncomplainingly the irritations and difficulties of rationing.

By the end of 1945 the United Nations Relief and Rehabilitation Agency (UNRRA) was administering five hundred million pounds' worth of relief supplies in twenty different countries. Many thought the contribution made by the British government was insufficient.

Beyond the immediate bleak aspect of western Europe there seemed hope of an exciting future, and Winston Churchill pointed the way. He was given a wildly enthusiastic reception when he visited Brussels in November. He told a joint session of the Belgian parliament: "I see no reason why, under the guardianship of a world organisation, there should not arise a united states of Europe, which would ultimately unify this continent in a manner never known since the fall of the Roman Empire . . .". Such aspirations were echoed on many public platforms. In Norwich Colonel Frank Medlicott, MP, told a Conservative audience that he favoured Mr Churchill's proposal for a Council of Europe, and he coupled this vision of Europe with the idea of a welfare state in Britain. In this country, he said, he wanted employment for all, social insurance, a national nutritional policy that would ensure a reasonable standard of food for every child and a great rehousing scheme. It sounded as if there was a perpetual Christmas just around the corner.

The first peacetime Christmas season was indeed at hand, and every effort was made to give it special significance. In Norwich the Christmas Fair returned to the cattle market with all its lights ablaze and the roundabouts, galloping horses and cake-walks freshly painted. The Food Ministry found extra rations for

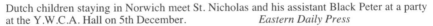

Dutch children staying in Norwich meet St. Nicholas and his assistant Black Peter at a party at the Y.W.C.A. Hall on 5th December.   *Eastern Daily Press*

Christmas week: a pound of sugar, four ounces of chocolates and sweets, six ounces of butter and margarine, six-pennyworth of carcase meat and four-pennyworth of corned beef. All the East Anglian market towns were crowded and their atmosphere was lively. Poultry farmers flocked in with birds for the festive table. The *Eastern Daily Press* reported: "Nearly every motor and horse-drawn vehicle arriving carried crates of prime stock, some openly and others covered with tarpaulins."

The birds did not get into the auctioneers' pens, which would normally have been full of thousands of head of poultry. The government had imposed price controls—2s 2d a pound for turkeys and 1s 2d a pound for prime chickens and hens—and so the farmers sold in private deals at twice the controlled price. That this happened all over East Anglia was later shown when magistrates imposed stiff fines on those who were caught. A Conservative MP declared in the Commons that the whole production of turkeys in East Anglia had gone into the black market. A Labour Member, citing experience at Diss, said farmers had taken live birds to market and sold them to so-called "stock breeders". In ninety-nine per cent of cases the birds found their way to hotels and restaurants.

So the new world of high ideals and noble intentions had not eliminated the darker side of human nature, and the formulae for ensuring fair shares for all were found to be imperfect. Old virtues survived and offered hope for the future. Essential characteristics re-emerged: in Cambridge, cosmopolitan and eclectic; in Norwich, shrewdly mercantile with a strong undercurrent of radical dissent; in Ipswich, determinedly agrarian but sinewy with industry; in the rural countryside, still moving with the rhythms of nature but with a new self-confidence.

King George VI, who spent Christmas with the Royal Family at Sandringham—their first Christmas there since 1938—could reasonably offer those who heard his Christmas Day broadcast "a future with hope". He called on the young to "bring now all that fine spirit to make it one of joyous adventure, a home where men and women can live in mutual trust and walk together as friends".

Appendix

Results of General Election on 5th July 1945

*Details in small type give results in the previous general election, in 1935,
or in any subsequent by-election*

Cambridgeshire

CAMBRIDGE BOROUGH:
Major A. L. Symonds (Lab.)		19,671
Lieutenant Commander Richard L. Tufnell (Con.)		18,989
Lieutenant Commander Richard L. Tufnell (Nat. Con.)	18,927	
Dr. W. A. Wood (Lab.)	13,436	

CAMBRIDGE UNIVERSITY (2 seats):
Sir Kenneth Pickthorn (Con.)		7,364
H. Wilson Harris (Ind.)		6,556
J. B. Priestley (Ind. Prog.)		5,745
Sir John Withers (Con.)	7,602	
Sir Kenneth Pickthorn (Con.)	6,917	
H. L. Elvin (Lab.)	3,453	

CAMBRIDGESHIRE:
A. E. Stubbs (Lab.)		18,714
G. Howard (Con.)		18,670
Lieutenant L. E. Goodman (Lib.)		6,867
Captain Richard G. Briscoe (Con.)	19,087	
Major J. R. Bellerby (Lab.)	11,437	
J. W. Payne (Lib.)	5,223	

ISLE OF ELY:
Major E. A. H. Legge-Bourke (Con.)		15,592
Lieutenant Commander A. Gray (Lab.)		13,271
James de Rothschild (Lib.)		9,564
James de Rothschild (Lib.)	17,671	
W. F. C. Carthwaite (Con.)	16,972	

HUNTINGDONSHIRE:
Major D. L. Renton (Lib. Nat.)		15,389
W. A. Waters (Lab.)		9,458
H. D. Walston (Lib.)		5,869
Dr. Sidney J. Peters (Lib. Nat.)	17,287	
L. J. George (Lab.)	7,861	

Norfolk

NORWICH (2 SEATS):
Lady Noel-Buxton (Lab.)		31,553
John Paton (Lab.)		31,229
Sir Geoffrey Shakespeare, Bt (Lib. Nat.)		25,945
Henry G. Strauss (Con.)		24,225
Sir Geoffrey Shakespeare, Bt (Lib. Nat.)	36,039	
Henry G. Strauss (Con.)	34,182	
W. G. Hall (Lab.)	24,670	
C. J. Kelly (Lab.)	22,055	
Fenner Brockway (I.L.P.)	6,737	

EAST NORFOLK:
Brigadier Frank Medlicott (Lib. Nat.)		23,307
N. R. Tillett (Lab.)		18,467
(by-election 26.1.39)		
Frank Medlicott (Lib. Nat.)	18,257	
N. R. Tillett (Lab.)	10.785	

NORTH NORFOLK:
E. G. Gooch (Lab.)		17,753
Sir Thomas Cook (Con.)		12,507
Sir Thomas Cook (Con.)	17,863	
Lady Noel-Buxton (Lab.)	14,465	

SOUTH NORFOLK:
Major C. P. Mayhew (Lab.)		16,825
Colonel J. S. Allen (Con.)		10,862
Major J. H. Wilson (Ind. Con.)		5,761
James A. Christie (Con.)	18,420	
G. Clark (Lab.)	13,409	

SOUTH-WEST NORFOLK:
S. Dye (Lab.)		15,091
Captain Somerset de Chair (Con.)		15,038
Somerset de Chair (Con.)	16,060	
S. Dye (Lab.)	11,943	

KING'S LYNN:
Major F. J. Wise (Lab.)		18,202
Donald McCullogh (Con.)		14,928
A. P. D. Penrose (Lib.)		3,796
Commander G. Bowles (Ind.)		444
(by-election 12.2.43)		
Lord Fermoy (Con.)	10,696	
Major F. J. Wise (Ind. Soc.)	9,027	

EAST ANGLIA 1945

GREAT YARMOUTH:
Squadron Leader E. Kinghorn (Lab.)		10,079
P. W. Jewson (Lib. Nat.)		7,974
(by election 8.4.41)		
P. W. Jewson (Lib. Nat.)		unopposed

Soke of Peterborough

PETERBOROUGH:
S. Tiffany (Lab.)		22,056
Viscount Suirdale (Con.)		21,485
(by-election 15.10.43)		
Viscount Suirdale (Con.)	11,976	
S. Bennett (Ind.)	10,890	

Suffolk

BURY ST EDMUNDS:
Lieutenant Colonel G. B. Clifton Brown (Con.)		15,013
Miss C. McCall (Lab.)		9,195
H. C. Drayton (Lib.)		2,863
E. C. Gordon England (Common Wealth)		750
(by election 22.2.44)		
Major E. M. Keatinge (Con.)	11,705	
Mrs M. Corbett Ashby (Ind. Lib.)	9,121	

EYE:
Edgar Granville (Lib.)		11,899
Major A. M. Borthwick (Con.)		10,950
B. Collingson (Lab.)		8,089
Edgar Granville	21,606	
H. L. Self (Lab.)	7,613	

IPSWICH:
Richard R. Stokes (Lab.)		26,296
F. G. G. Fison (Con.)		18,177
Major D. M. S. Mowat (Lib.)		8,819
(by-election 16.2.38)		
Richard R. Stokes (Lab.)	27,604	
H. U. Willink (Nat. Con.)	24,443	

LOWESTOFT:
E. Evans (Lab.)		12,759
Pierse C. Loftus (Con.)		10,996
Lieutenant M. P. Crosse (Lib.)		6,545
Pierse C. Loftus (Con.)	21,064	
Major F. J. Wise (Lab.)	13,348	

SUDBURY:
Lieutenant Colonel R. Hamilton (Lab.) 9,906
Colonel Henry W. Burton (Con.) 9,659
Mrs M. Hitchcock (Lib.) 5,045
  Colonel Henry W. Burton (Con.) 11,700
  A. J. Sainsbury (Lib.) 8,344
  Lieutenant Commander H. Denton (Lab.) 3,670

WOODBRIDGE
Lieutenant Colonel John Hare (Con.) 16,073
J. M. Stewart (Lab.) 11,380
Captain D. B. Law (Lib.) 6,740
  Walter Ross-Taylor (Con.) 22,715
  A. V. Smith (Lab.) 8,808

Essex
CHELMSFORD:
Wing Commander E.R. Millington (Common Wealth) 27,309
Hubert Ashton (Con.) 25,229
Miss H. Buckmaster (Lib.) 5,909
  (by-election 26.4.45)
  Wing Commander E.R. Millington (Common Wealth) 24,548
  Flight Lieutenant Brian Cook (Con.) 18,117

COLCHESTER:
Captain C. Smith (Lab.) 16,587
Oswald Lewis (Con.) 14,123
Captain G. A. Routledge (Lib.) 5,899
  Oswald Lewis (Con.) 19,915
  H. Beaumont (Lab.) 14,039

HARWICH:
Sir J. Stanley Holmes (Lib. Nat.) 16,452
J. Hewett (Lab.) 13,067
  J. Stanley Holmes (Lib. Nat.) 21,716
  A. E. Appelbe (Lab.) 9,170

MALDON:
Tom Driberg (Lab.) 22,480
Major M. Stevenson (Con.) 14,753
  (by-election 25.6.42)
  Tom Driberg (Ind.) 12,219
  R. J. Hunt (Con.) 6,626
  B. Matthews (Ind.) 1,476

SAFFRON WALDEN:
Rt Hon. R .A. Butler (Con.) 16,950
S. S. Wilson (Lab.) 15,792
G. Edinger (Lib.) 3,395
  R. A. Butler (Con.) 19,669
  Mrs C. D. Rackham (Lab.) 9,633

Notes on Sources

A principal source has been, as for previous volumes in this series, the regional newspapers, and particularly the *Eastern Daily Press*, the *East Anglian Daily Times* and the *Cambridge Daily News*. Several definitive works of military history have provided the information about the experiences of the East Anglian regiments. Similarly the activity on British and American air bases has been well documented in a number of authoritative works, which have been freely drawn upon.

The various volumes of the official *History of the Second World War*, published by Her Majesty's Stationery Office, have been used as a source for the background of national and international events, supplemented by Sir Winston Churchill's personal account and the histories produced by Martin Gilbert.

The Mass Observation Archive at Sussex University has provided information about the day-to-day experiences and thoughts of civilians living in East Anglia.

Full acknowledgement of these sources is made below, and references given where appropriate.

Introduction and Acknowledgements

(1) John Comer: *Combat Crew—The Story of 25 Combat Missions over North-West Europe*, Leo Cooper Ltd, 1988.

Chapter One

(1) Martin Gilbert: *Road to Victory—Winston S. Churchill, 1941–1945*, page 1182. Heinemann, 1986 (quoting Sarah Churchill: *Keep on Dancing*, pages 75–77).
(2) Mass Observation Diaries, Ref. S5205.
(3) Mass Observation Diaries, Ref. C5271.
(4) James Good Brown: *The Mighty Men of the 381st, Heroes All*, pages 574–575. Publishers Press, Salt Lake City, 1984.
(5) Michael J. F. Bowyer: *Air Raid! The Enemy Air Offensive against East Anglia, 1939–45*, Page 333, Patrick Stephens, 1986.
(6) John T. Appleby: *Suffolk Summer*, page 48. East Anglian Magazine Ltd, 1952.
(7) Mass Observation Diaries, Ref. S5205.
(8) Appleby, *op. cit.*, page 19.
(9) Robert Kee: *1945—The World We Fought For*, page 253, (quoting an Associated Press eye-witness). Hamish Hamilton, 1985.

Chapter Two

(1) M. R. D. Foot & J. M. Langley: *M19—Escape and Evasion, 1939–1945*, page 296. Bodley Head, 1979.
(2) B. A. Stait: *Rivenhall—The History of an Essex Airfield*, pages 48–51, Alan Sutton Publishing Ltd, 1984.
(3) Sir Charles Webster & Noble Frankland: *The Strategic Air Offensive against Germany*, pages 55–56. HMSO, 1961.
(4) Normal Longmate: *The Bombers—The RAF Offensive against Germany, 1939–45*, Hutchinson, 1983.

(5) Dennis Richards : *Portal of Hungerford,* pages 318–324. Heinemann, 1978.

(6) Webster & Frankland, *op. cit.,* vol. 4, page 172; Longmate, *op. cit.,* page 330.

(7) Longmate, *op. cit.,* page 330.

(8) Ibid., pages 325–327.

(9) Ibid., page 327.

(10) Ibid., pages 327–328.

(11) Martin Middlebrook & Chris Everitt: *The Bomber Command War Diaries—an Operational Reference Book, 1939–1945,* page 646. Viking, 1985.

(12) Ibid., page 658.

(13) Brown: *op.cit.,*

(14) Middlebrook & Everitt, *op. cit.,* pages 647–648.

(15) Sir Arthur Harris: *Bomber Offensive,* page 238. Collins, 1947.

(16) Longmate: *op. cit.,* page 332

(17) Gilbert: *op.cit.,*

(18) Longmate, *op. cit.,* page 339.

(19) Ibid., page 341.

(20) Webster & Frankland, *op. cit.* vol. 3, pages 117–119.

(21) PRO, Ref ATH/DO/4B.

(22) Webster & Frankland, *op. cit.,* vol. 3, pages 117–119.

(23) Middlebrook & Everitt, *op. cit.,* pages 671–672.

(24) Brown, *op. cit.,* pages 577–580.

(25) Ibid., page 579.

(26) Martin Bowman: *Fields of Little America,* page 104. Wensum Books, 1977.

(27) Middlebrook & Everitt, *op. cit.,* pages 673, 678 and 683.

(28) Ibid., page 678.

(29) Bowman, *op. cit.,* page 104.

(30) Ibid., page 104.

(31) Middlebrook & Everitt, *op. cit.,* pages 703–704.

Chapter Three

(1) Colonel T. A. Martin: *The Essex Regiment, 1929–50,* page 233. The Essex Regiment Association, 1952.

(2) Lieutenant Commander P. K. Kemp: *The History of the Royal Norfolk Regiment, 1919–1951,* page 54. The Regimental Association of the Royal Norfolk Regiment, 1953.

(3) Norman Scarfe: *Assault Division, A History of the 3rd Division from the Invasion of Normandy to the Surrender of Germany,* page 206. Collins, 1947.

(4) Mass Observation Diaries, Ref. S5205.

(5) Scarfe, *op. cit.,* page 223.

(6) Ibid., page 226.

(7) G. J. Scriven: *Called Up,* page 39. Published by the author, nd.

(8) Scarfe, *op. cit.,* page 243.

(9) Martin, *op. cit.,* page 238.

(10) Ibid., page 424.

Chapter Four

(1) Martin Gilbert: *Second World War,* page 642. Weidenfeld & Nicolson, 1989.

(2) Ibid., page 695.

(3) Ibid., pages 659–660.

(4) Robert Kee: *op. cit.*, page 322.

(5) Ibid., page 324.

(6) Gilbert, *op. cit.*, page 709.

(7) Kee, *op. cit.*, page 325.

(8) Colonel W. N. Nicholson: *The Suffolk Regiment,* 1928–46. page 227. East Anglian Magazine, nd.

(9) Ibid.

(10) Michael Moore: *Battalion at War—Singapore 1942*, Page 109, Gliddon Books, Norwich, 1988.

(11) Ibid., page 109.

(12) Ibid., page 109.

(13) Nicholson, *op. cit.*, page 246.

(14) Ibid., page 247.

Chapter Five

(1) Mass Observation, Ref. "Directive Replies", September 1944.

(2) Ibid.

(3) Ibid., May 1945.

(4) Mass Observation Diaries, Ref. S5205.

(5) Mass Observation Diaries, Ref. C5271.

(6) Brown: *op. cit.*,page 611.

(7) Appleby: *op. cit.*,pages 51–52.

(8) Gilbert: *Second World War, op. cit.*, page 694. Weidenfeld & Nicholson, 1989.

(9) Hervey Benham (ed.): *Essex at War*, pages 86–87. Benhams of Colchester, 1945.

(10) Mass Observation Diaries, Ref. S5205.

(11) Michael J. F. Bowyer: pages 327 and 330.

(12) Ibid., page 330.

Chapter Six

(1) Mass Observation Diaries, Ref. C5271.

(2) Mass Observation Diaries, Ref. S5205.

(3) Stait: *op. cit.*, page 49.

(4) Mass Observation, Ref: "Directive Replies', June 1945.

(5) Appleby: *op. cit.*, pages 111–112.

Chapter Seven

(1) Quoted by Norman Longmate: *The G.I's—The Americans in Britain, 1942–45,* page 322. Hutchinson, 1975.

(2) Brown: *op. cit.*, page 611.

(3) Ibid., page 621.

(4) Appleby: *op. cit.*, pages 20–21.

(5) Gilbert: *Second World War*, *op. cit.*, page 692.

(6) Gilbert: *The Road to Victory—Winston S. Churchill, 1941–1945, op. cit.*, page 1,167.

(7) Foot & Langley: *op. cit.*, page 294.

(8) Nicholson: *op. cit.*, pages 146–147.

(9) Martin: *op. cit.*, page 240.

(10) Mass Observation Diaries, Ref. C5271.
(11) Miriam Kochan: *Prisoners of England,* page 103, Macmillan, 1980.
(12) Matthew Barry Sullivan: *Thresholds of Peace—Four Hundred Thousand German Prisoners and the People of Britain, 1944–48,* page 94. Hamish Hamilton, 1979.
(13) Kochan, *op. cit.*, page 104.
(14) Ibid., page 104.
(15) Ibid., pages 116 and 125.

Chapter Eight

(1) Appleby: *op. cit.,* page 86.
(2) Nicholson *op cit.*, page 146.
(3) Ibid., page 148.
(4) Martin: *op. cit.,* page 338.

Chapter Nine

(1) Ken Rice: *Ipswich, An Illustrated History of Ipswich Town Football Club*, Wensum Books, nd.

Chapter Ten

(1) Mass Observation, Ref. "Directive Replies", June 1944.
(2) Mass Observation Diaries, Ref. C5271.
(3) Ministry of Agriculture national figures, quoted in *Eastern Daily Press*, 12th May, 1945.
(4) Mass Observation, Ref. "Directive Replies", June 1944.
(5) Ibid.
(6) Gilbert, *Second World War*, *op. cit.,* page 646.
(7) Ibid., page 658.
(8) Ibid., page 680.
(9) Gilbert, *The Road to Victory—Winston S. Churchill 1941–1945*, *op. cit.*, page 1,332.

Errata

The author is indebted to readers of earlier volumes in this series who have written describing their own experiences during the war and have drawn attention to the following inaccuracies in my text.

EAST ANGLIA 1940

Page 49, line 13—Read "Norfolk Yeomanry" instead of "Royal Norfolks". The Norfolk Yeomanry (King's Own Royal Regiment) was part of the Royal Artillery.

Page 106, lines 8 to 11—Amend sentence to read: "Only minutes later, two anti-aircraft gunners at Martlesham picked up a single plane in their predictor lens, flying so high that they could not identify it. When it was almost overhead they saw something appear beneath it, and realized that bombs were being aimed at the airfield. Thirteen fell in a straight line along the edge of the airfield, the last one damaging the refrigerator plant."

EAST ANGLIA 1941

Page 89, lines 13 to 15—amend to read: ". . . on 15th February Norwich City played West Ham, holders of the Football League War Cup (which had been competed for the first time in the previous season), at Carrow Road and won 2–1."

Page 118, lines 3 and 4—amend to read: ". . . and the battleship *Barham* was also sunk in the Mediterranean by another U-boat, with the loss of 861 lives."

EAST ANGLIA 1942

Page 58, last two lines—amend to read: "At 9.30 pm on 12th June a solitary Dornier flew over the town and released a stick of bombs."

Page 59, lines 3 and 4—amend to read: ". . . forty-two people were killed, seventeen of them civilians and the others Service personnel".

Pages 135, final paragraph—The riddle of whether the couple who went through a marriage ceremony at Quy in April 1942 became man and wife was eventually solved a year later. The *East Anglian Daily Times* reported on 24th February 1943: "Church and legal circles do not consider the ceremony was a marriage and since the parties are not married, no steps need to be taken towards a divorce or annulling the ceremony."

EAST ANGLIA 1943

Page 75, last line, and page 76, first 3 lines—amend to read: ". . . carried what had formerly been the 7th Battalion of the Suffolk Regiment but had now been metamorphozed into the 142nd Regiment of the Royal Armoured Corps. From their traditional infantry role the Suffolk men had changed in November 1941 . . .".

Page 77, last line—amend to read: "The Suffolk men of the 142nd Regiment, Royal Armoured Corps . . ."

Page 78, last line—amend to read: "Both the Essex and the Suffolk regiments played a part . . .".

Page 79, lines 4, 6 and 18: in each case amend "Cambridgeshire men" to read "Suffolk men".

EAST ANGLIA 1944

Page 23, picture caption—should read "Horsham".

Page 164, picture caption—should read "Operation Manna".

Selected Bibiliography

Volumes in the official *History of the Second World War*, published by HMSO:
  Captain S. W. Roskill: *The War at Sea, 1939–45*, 3 vols., 1959–61.
  H. St G. Saunders: *The R.A.F., 1939–45*, vol 3: *The Fight is Won*, 1954.
W. S. Churchill: *The Second World War*, vols. V and VI, Cassell, 1952 and 1954.
Basil Collier: *A Short History of the Second World War*, Collins, 1967.
Martin Gilbert: *Road to Victory—Winston S. Churchill 1941–1945*, Heinemann, 1986.
Martin Gilbert: *Second World War*, Weidenfeld & Nicolson, 1989.

Lieutenant Commander P. K. Kemp, RN: *History of the Royal Norfolk Regiment,* vol. III, 1919–1951. Regimental Association 1953.
Colonel T. A. Martin: *The Essex Regiment, 1929–50*, The Essex Regimental Association, 1952.
Colonel W. N. Nicholson: *The Suffolk Regiment, 1928–46,* East Anglian Magazine, nd.
Norman Scarfe: *Assault Division—A History of the 3rd Division, from the Invasion of Normandy to the Surrender of Germany,* Collins, 1947.

Martin Bowman: *Fields of Little America,* Wensum Books, 1977.
Michael J. F. Bowyer: *Action Stations—Wartime Military Airfields of East Anglia, 1939–45,* Patrick Stephens, 1979.
James Good Brown: *The Might Men of the 381st Heroes All,* Publishers' Press, Salt Lake City, Utah 84119, 1984.
Roger Freeman: *The Mighty Eighth,* Macdonald, 1970.
Roger Freeman: *Mighty Eighth—War Diary,* Janes, 1981.
Max Hastings: *Bomber Command,* Michael Joseph, 1979.
Ken Merrick: *By Day and by Night—The Bomber War in Europe, 1939–45,* Ian Allan Ltd, 1989.
Martin Middlebrook & Chris Everitt: *The Bomber Command War Diaries—An Operational Reference Book, 1939–1945,* Viking, 1985.
W. Ramsey: *Airfields of the Eighth—Then & Now*, B of B Prints International, 1978.
B. A. Stait: *Rivenhall—The History of an Essex Airfield,* Alan Sutton Publishing Ltd, 1984.

John T. Appleby: *Suffolk Summer*, East Anglian Magazine, 1948 (several reprints).
Hervey Benham (ed.); *Essex at War*, Benhams of Colchester, 1945.
Michael J.F. Bowyer: *Air Raid! The Enemy Air Offensive against East Anglia, 1939–45,* Patrick Stephens, 1986.
East Suffolk County Council: *Civil Defence in East Suffolk,* Ipswich 1948.
Harry G. Hitchman & Philip Driver: *HMS Badger—5 Years in the Front Line,* published by the authors, Harwich, 1945.
Ford Jenkins: *Port War: Lowestoft at War 1939–45*, W.S. Cowell, Ipswich, nd.
Robert Kee: *1945—The World We Fought For*, Hamish Hamilton, 1985.
Miriam Kochan: *Prisoners of England,* Macmillan, 1980.
Norman Longmate: *The G.I's—The Americans In Britain, 1942–45*, Hutchinson, 1975.
Norfolk County Council: *The War in Norfolk—Report of the Chief Constable, 1945.*

Index

(Illustrations in bold type)

	National and International	*Regional*
October:	UNO formally established. Charter of UN Food and Agricultural Organisation signed. First ex-prisoners of war from Far East return to UK. Text published of Bill to nationalise Bank of England.	Joyous reception of local men returning from Japanese prison camps. 500 Dutch children received into Norfolk homes for 8 weeks visit. Drifters begin fishing—Scots "fisher-girls" reappear in ports.
November:	Nuremberg trial of Nazi war criminals opens. Protest strikes and demonstrations by Arabs against Balfour Declaration. de Gaulle forms three-party French government. Attlee US Congress and Canadian Parliament. UK government announces five-year nationalisation plan.	Municipal elections confirm swing to left; Labour Mayors elected. Cambridge University honours war leaders. Campaigns for "European Relief" in Norwich and Cambridge. Resorts seek financial aid from government to help revive. Cambridge undergraduates vote that "Britain has taken road to serfdom".
December:	Moscow conference of foreign ministers of UK, Russia and the USA to discuss peace treaties. Financial agreement between UK and USA signed. Chiang Kai-shek re-enters Nanking. UK Coal Industry Nationalisation Bill issued.	Royal Family's first Christmas at Sandringham since 1939. East Anglians accused of running poultry "black market".